CLASSI

The *Friendly* Guide to

Mozart

Darren Henley & Tim Lihoreau

Hodder Arnold

www.hoddereducation.com

For UK order enquiries: please contact Bookpoint Ltd, 130 Milton Park, Abingdon, Oxon OX14 4SB. Telephone: +44(0) 1235 827720. Fax: +44(0) 1235 400454. Lines are open 09.00–18.00, Monday to Saturday, with a 24-hour message answering service. You can also order through our website www.hoddereducation.com

British Library Cataloguing in Publication Data: a catalogue record for this title is available from the British Library.

First published in UK 2005, by Hodder Education, 338 Euston Road, London NW1 3BH.

Typeset by Servis Filmsetting Ltd, Manchester
Printed in Great Britain for Hodder Education, a division of Hodder Headline, 338 Euston Road, London NW1 3BH, by Cox & Wyman Ltd, Reading, Berkshire.

Hodder Headline's policy is to use papers that are natural, renewable and recyclable products and made from wood grown in sustainable forests. The logging and manufacturing processes are expected to conform to the environmental regulations of the country of origin.

Impression number   10 9 8 7 6 5 4 3 2 1

Year   2010 2009 2008 2007 2006 2005

"If only the whole world could feel the power of harmony."

Wolfgang Amadeus Mozart

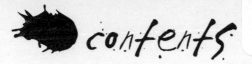 contents

Introduction viii

A Friendly Word Before We Get Started . . . xii

01 The Friendly Guide to What Was
    Composed When 1

02 The Story of Mozart: The Cast List 15

03 The Boy Genius 23

04 On the Road 31

05 The Adult Composer 91

06 The Final Year 117

07 Opera Plots 135

08 Have a Listen Yourself 163

09 Mozart's Movie Music 177

10 What the Others Said About Mozart . . . 181

11 Where to Find Out More 185

Mozart Mood Chart 189

Index 190

About the Authors 193

Introduction

Wolfgang Amadeus Mozart is arguably the greatest
composer who ever lived. In the 250 years since
he died, the popularity of his music has soared and
he is now recognized around the world as being at
the top of the classical music tree.

This book is not intended to be a scholarly or
academic guide to his life and compositions – there
are plenty of those in the bookshops already.
Instead, in the first chapters of *The Classic FM
Friendly Guide to Mozart*, we aim to take you by the
hand and provide you with, well, a *friendly*
introduction to the man behind the music. In later
chapters of the book, we explore many of the
greatest pieces that he wrote. In true Classic FM

style, we have removed as much of the jargon that sometimes surrounds classical music as we possibly can. So, once you have finished reading this slim volume, we guarantee that you will be able to hold your own in a dinner party conversation with any self-proclaimed classical music expert.

You will find a CD inside the cover that includes excerpts from Mozart's Top 20 hits, as voted by listeners to the Classic FM Hall of Fame, our annual poll to discover the UK's favourite classical music. Each year since we began compiling the chart in 1996, Mozart has had more entries than any other composer. Once you have enjoyed his 20 best-known pieces, we have made some suggestions of further Mozart works that you might like to hunt out and give a listen to.

There's no getting away from it – Mozart wrote some great tunes. In fact, if you listen to any of his pieces of music, the tunes are bursting to get out left, right and centre. He himself wrote that *"Melody is the very essence of music"* and this is the secret of his success. He had a knack of creating music that stays with you in your memory bank as soon as you first hear it. He was very clear in his own mind about the sort of music that he wrote:

I pay no attention whatever to anybody's praise or blame. I simply follow my own feelings.

He was also completely unashamed about writing music that was easy to listen to:

Nevertheless, the passions whether violent or not, should never be so expressed as to reach the point of causing disgust; and music, even in situations of the greatest horror, should never be painful to the ear but should flatter and charm it, and thereby always remain music.

Mozart was incredibly prolific during his tragically short life, especially considering the amount of time he spent touring and teaching so that he could pay the bills. He himself said *"I write as a sow piddles"* and in the 35 years of his life he composed more than 650 works. He proved that he could turn his hand to any type of music. He was equally comfortable writing symphonies as he was composing operas and he excelled at creating choral masterpieces, just as he did when it came to penning piano concertos.

There is one question about Mozart that has constantly occurred to us while we have been working on this book – what more might he have achieved had he lived for longer than 35 years? The answer is unimaginable, but we're reminded of the words of the American songwriter and entertainer, Tom Lehrer: "It is a sobering thought . . . that when Mozart was my age he had been dead for two years."

Darren Henley
Tim Lihoreau
Classic FM, November 2005

A Friendly Word Before We Get Started ...

As you might expect, this book contains many references to pieces of music. We wanted to make our guide to Mozart as friendly on the eye as possible, so we have decided to simplify the rules about how pieces of music appear:

- titles of all musical works are set in italics
- songs and arias appear in italics within quotation marks.

Mozart's music was catalogued after his death by one Ludwig von Köchel, who rather self-effacingly decided to give each of Mozart's works a Köchel number to show the order in which his music was published. We have decided to omit the Köchel number in the main body of our text, unless there are two Mozart pieces with identical names, in which case, you will find the letter "K" (for Köchel) and a number following the italicized title. Don't be put off – it may sound complicated, but we promise, it's the friendly way to do it.

The Friendly Guide to What Was Composed When

It is easy for us to think of composers writing music in isolation, but it is very unusual for that to actually be the case. Many of Mozart's greatest works were written because of financial need, or because of a particular job he held at a particular time, rather than out of a desire to be creative for creativity's sake.

The chronology starting overleaf allows you to work out what was written when – and also put the events in Mozart's life into some sort of historical context.

It would be impossible to detail all 655 of his works, so we have picked out some of the highlights from each year.

YEAR	What was happening to Mozart?	What was Mozart composing?	What else was going on in the world?
1756	Mozart is born on 27 January in Salzburg. He is his parents' seventh child, but is only the second one to actually survive	He may have been prodigious, but it will be a few years yet before Mozart gets going on the composing front	The Seven Years' War begins with England and Prussia on one side and Austria and France on the other
1757			Clive conquers Bengal
1758			Horatio Nelson is born
1759			The renowned British canal builder, James Brindley, designs the Worsley–Manchester canal
1760			George III ascends to the throne following the death of his grandfather, George II
1761	His musical education is underway. At the beginning of the year, he learns to play his first piece on the piano, by the now little-known composer, Wagenseil. He also makes his first public performance, in Salzburg	It doesn't take long for Mozart to begin composing. His first piece is called *Andante for Piano*	William Pitt resigns

CONTINUED ▶

YEAR	What was happening to Mozart?	What was Mozart composing?	What else was going on in the world?
1762	Mozart and his sister Nannerl are turning into a good double act. They have royal command performances in both Munich and Vienna	He's spreading his wings now in composition terms, writing his first violin sonatas. Remember, he's still only 6 years old	In Russia, Catherine II (The Great) becomes Tsarina, deposing her husband, Tzar Peter
1763	They're off on their first European tour. This year, they take in Munich, Frankfurt, Brussels and Paris	More violin sonatas	The Seven Years' War ends
1764	The tour continues with more performances for royalty: King Louis XV in Paris and King George III in London	Yet more violin sonatas, but he also finds time to write his first symphony. Mozart's first pieces of music are actually published. He's now reached the grand old age of 8	James Hargreaves invents the Spinning Jenny
1765	Stays in London for the first half of the year, before travelling to The Hague to perform for Prince William V of Orange. Their journey takes them via Canterbury, Dover, Calais, Lille and Antwerp. Ill with intestinal typhoid	By the end of this year, he's already up to *Symphony No. 5*	Emperor Francis Stephen dies and is replaced by his son, who becomes Emperor Joseph II

1766	The concerts continue, with dates this year in Utrecht, Amsterdam, Antwerp, Brussels, Paris, Dijon, Lyon, Lausanne, Zurich and Munich. Just before the end of the year, the family finally arrives home in Salzburg	He writes yet more violin sonatas this year	The English scientist, Henry Cavendish, proves that hydrogen is an element
1767	The family are back on the road; this time to Vienna and Bohemia. Mozart is seriously ill again, after being struck down by smallpox	He wins a gold medal and a cash prize for his cantata, *Die Schuldigkeit des ersten Gebots*. The symphony tally is now up to six	The Jesuits are expelled from Spain
1768	Mozart spends the year going backwards and forwards between Vienna and Salzburg	The work rate is increasing with a couple of operas and *Symphonies No. 7* and *No. 8* being premiered this year	The Royal Academy of Arts is founded in London
1769	Towards the end of this year, Mozart is given the job of concertmaster at the Salzburg court. There's no money involved, but it's definitely a step up. He goes on the road to Innsbruck and then to Verona	Among the music Mozart writes, in his first year as a teenager, are three cassations. These are light, frothy pieces of music for a small group of musicians, which are often intended to be played outside	The Duke of Wellington and Napoleon Bonaparte are both born this year. They are destined to be linked again much later in life

CONTINUED ▶

YEAR	What was happening to Mozart?	What was Mozart composing?	What else was going on in the world?
1770	Life as an itinerant musician continues. This year, Mozart performs in Verona, Milan, Bologna, Florence, Rome and Naples	Musical highlights this year include a clutch of symphonies and an opera	James Cook discovers New South Wales, landing at Botany Bay
1771	Mozart spends spring in Venice before finally returning to Salzburg again. He's only at home for about 4 months, before he's off to Italy for the rest of the year	Yet more operatic work – but none of the big ones. On the symphony front, he is now up to *No. 14*. Not a bad effort for somebody who is just celebrating his 16th birthday	Sir Walter Scott, the Scottish novelist, is born in Edinburgh
1772	Things are looking up – Mozart is appointed concertmaster in Salzburg, with a salary this time. His boss is pretty understanding, though, allowing him time off to spend a couple of months in Milan	A couple more operas under his belt. It's also a big year for symphonies, with no fewer than seven being published. He's starting to write more divertimenti (lighter pieces of music) and also has three string quartets published	The first partition of Poland, with Russia, Prussia and Austria making the divisions
1773	There's a new, bigger home in Salzburg for the Mozart family. Meanwhile, Wolfgang fancies the idea of a job in Vienna, but a	Mozart writes *Exsultate, jubilate* for Venanzio Rauzzini. These days, this is sung by a soprano, but Mr Rauzzini was a castrato. You could say he gave	The "Boston Tea Party" takes place

	meeting with the Empress draws a blank	up a lot for his art	
1774	He might be celebrating his 18th birthday, but there's still plenty of hard work to do, writing music for his boss, the Archbishop of Salzburg	He writes his *Bassoon Concerto*. Then, towards the end of the year, he's commissioned to write the opera *La finta giardiniera*	English chemist, Joseph Priestley, discovers oxygen
1775	Mozart begins the year in Munich for the premiere of *La finta giardiniera*. It's a big success and more performances of Mozart's other works follow. Still no big new job, though	The violin seems to be taking Mozart's fancy this year. He composes his first five *Violin Concertos*	The American War of Independence begins with the battle of Lexington
1776	Just for a change, a full year in Salzburg	Just because he wasn't travelling around, it didn't mean that Mozart's creative juices would stop flowing. This year, as well as composing his *Piano Concerto No. 8*, he also wrote a *Concerto for Three Pianos*	America declares its independence from Great Britain
1777	The travelling bug bites again. He's very grudgingly given time off by the Archbishop of Salzburg and	Before he sets off on his tour, he writes his *Piano Concerto No. 9 in E Flat*, for a rather mysterious French	D. Bushnell, an American engineer, invents the torpedo

CONTINUED ▶

YEAR	What was happening to Mozart?	What was Mozart composing?	What else was going on in the world?
	goes on a 16-month tour. This time, however, he travels with his mother rather than his father. They travel to Munich, Augsburg and Mannheim, where Mozart falls in love with Aloysia Weber. Despite his best efforts, there's no permanent job for him there, though	pianist called Mademoiselle Jeunehomme. She must have been a pretty mean player because it's a tough piece to play	
1778	Mozart and his mother travel on to Paris, where his music is well liked. Sadly, his mother dies and there really isn't much point in him staying on in Paris. He returns to Salzburg, travelling via Strasbourg, Mannheim and Munich, to where Aloysia Weber has moved. She finally tells him that she's not interested in love. This is not a good year on the personal front	It's a more rewarding year creatively than it is in Mozart's private life. He composes his *Flute and Harp Concerto* for a pupil who could play both the flute and the harp (although one presumes not both at the same time, unless she was a virtuosic contortionist too). It's a big year for the flute with a couple of Flute Concertos too	France joins the American War of Independence

1779	Things are looking up on the money front. He returns to Salzburg to take up the job of court organist, in addition to his old role as concertmaster. He has to work hard teaching, playing in church and composing both religious and secular music whenever it's required. But he is paid very well for his services	Highlights this year include the *Coronation Mass* and *Sinfonia Concertante* K364	English inventor, Samuel Crompton, creates the spinning mule
1780	By and large Mozart does as he's asked by the boss and writes the music that's expected of him. By the end of the year, he's off on his travels again, though. It's back to Munich for rehearsals of his new opera, *Idomeneo*	He writes his *Vesperae solennes de confessore* (*Solemn Vespers*) for a mixture of solo singers, chorus and orchestra. One of his most popular sacred pieces comes from this work – "*Laudate Dominum*", a setting in Latin of Psalm 116. The symphonies are still coming, although not as thick and fast as they were at one stage. This year sees his *Symphony No. 33* get its first performance	Empress Maria Theresa dies and Joseph II takes over sole power in Austria. He begins a series of wide-ranging reforms
1781	He's ordered back from Munich to join the staff of Archbishop	*Idomeneo* is well received in Munich. He writes the *Serenade No. 10 in*	The planet Uranus is discovered by Sir William Herschel

CONTINUED ▶

YEAR	What was happening to Mozart?	What was Mozart composing?	What else was going on in the world?
	Colloredo in Salzburg. But Mozart doesn't think much of his status alongside the servants. He asks to leave and is quite literally kicked out by the Archbishop's chief steward. Things are looking up on the romantic front, though. He falls for Constanze Weber, Aloysia's younger sister. He duels on the piano with Clementi	*B Flat for 13 Wind Instruments*. This piece is actually longer than any of his symphonies and requires two oboes, two clarinets, two basset-horns, two bassoons, four horns and a contrabassoon	
1782	Mozart finally gets the girl and wedding bells sound. He marries Constanze on 4 August	His new opera *Die Entführung aus dem Serail* (*The Abduction from the Harem*) is premiered. He begins writing the six *Haydn String Quartets Nos. 14–20*, which are dedicated to his friend, the composer Joseph Haydn. He also writes *Symphony No. 35 in D*, dedicated to his friends the Haffner family. (It's known as *The Haffner*)	William Pitt and Benjamin Franklin begin to negotiate peace
1783	It's a year of happiness and great sadness for Mozart. He's busy	Sometime earlier, when Constanze had fallen ill, Mozart promised to	Britain, France, Spain and the United States sign the Treaty of Versailles

	performing in the early part of the year. In June, his first son is born, only to die 2 months later	write a mass if she got better. She did and the result was the *Mass No. 18 in C minor*, known as *The Great*. He never actually finished it, but it was performed, with Constanze herself taking one of the main soprano roles
1784	Mozart is struck down with a serious attack of colic while listening to an opera in Vienna. A few weeks afterwards, his second son is born. Mozart becomes a freemason. His lodge is named 'Beneficence'	He writes his *String Quartet No. 17 in B Flat* (another of the *Haydn Quartets*). This is known as *The Hunt*, and when you hear it, it's easy to work out why, with the music clearly depicting the thrill of the chase and the sound of the hunters' horns	The English lexicographer, Dr Samuel Johnson, dies
1785	Mozart throws himself into life as a freemason. His father also joins a lodge in Vienna. Mozart is now becoming rather well known – by the end of the year his portrait is even featured on a Viennese calendar	This was a big year for Mozart's piano output. He wrote his *Piano Concerto No. 20 in D minor* (the first he had written in a minor key) and *Piano Concerto No. 21 in C*. This is known as the *Elvira Madigan*, after it was used in a Swedish film of this name in the 1960s. Mozart's music has already proved more long-lasting than the movie. He also finished his *Fantasia*	Edmund Cartwright invents the power loom

CONTINUED ▶

YEAR	What was happening to Mozart?	What was Mozart composing?	What else was going on in the world?
		and *Sonata in C minor*, which he had begun the previous year. Many people think that this is his greatest work for solo piano	
1786	Mozart spends the year conducting, performing and composing. His third son is born in October, but he dies just 1 month later	Another big piano year. He wrote his *Piano Concerto No. 23 in A* and his *Piano Concerto No. 24 in C minor* just weeks apart. It's remarkable to think that he managed this level of output, especially as he also wrote one of his greatest operas, *The Marriage of Figaro*, this year and had time for his *Symphony No. 38*, which is known as the *Prague Symphony*	Goya designs the tapestries *The Seasons*
1787	*The Marriage of Figaro* is a massive success in Prague, as is the *Prague Symphony*. Ludwig van Beethoven, then aged just 16, studies in Vienna with Mozart. Mozart's father Leopold, who had a huge influence on his career, dies in Salzburg.	His new opera, *Don Giovanni*, receives its premiere in Prague, where it is a big hit. Rumour has it that he forgot to write the overture until the night before its first performance. This year also saw Mozart writing what must surely be his most famous	The American Constitution is drafted

	piece of music – his *Serenade No. 13 in G*, better known as *Eine kleine Nachtmusik*, which translates as "a little night music"	*The Times* newspaper begins publication in London
1788	Constanze gives birth to a daughter, but she only lives to be 6 months old. Money continues to be a worry for the Mozart family	
	Despite success in Prague, *Don Giovanni* does not go down well with audiences in Vienna. Money really is very tight now and Mozart gets more and more heavily into debt	He may be finding things financially tough, but there is no shortage of creative equity in the bank. In a period of just 6 weeks, he writes no fewer than three symphonies: *Symphony No. 39 in E Flat*, *Symphony No. 40 in G minor* and *Symphony No. 41 in C*, which is known as the *Jupiter Symphony*
1789	Mozart is off on his travels again. As well as performing wherever he goes, he's also on the lookout for patrons who will commission new works from him. He visits Dresden, Leipzig, Potsdam, Berlin and Prague. Constanze gives birth to a baby girl who, like her elder sister and two of her three elder brothers, dies while still an infant	Mozart wrote his *Clarinet Quintet in A* this year. It was inspired by his friend Anton Stadler, who was the principal clarinettist of the Imperial Court Orchestra of Vienna	The French Revolution begins, with the Bastille being stormed on 14 July

CONTINUED ▶

YEAR	What was happening to Mozart?	What was Mozart composing?	What else was going on in the world?
1790	Emperor Joseph II dies and Mozart journeys to Frankfurt for the coronation of his replacement, Leopold II. He gives concerts in Frankfurt, Mainz and Munich, but times are still hard financially	A new opera, *Così fan tutte*, has its premiere	The first lifeboat is built
1791	Mozart's sixth child is born – a boy; he becomes only the second to survive to adulthood. Mozart becomes ill towards the end of November and final rehearsals for his *Requiem* take place beside his bed. He dies in the early hours of 5 December. It's believed that he suffered from rheumatic inflammatory fever. He is buried in an unmarked grave just outside Vienna	The last year of Mozart's life is remarkable for the sheer number of masterpieces that he manages to write. His last public performance is of his new *Piano Concerto No. 27 in B Flat* in March. He writes the motet *Ave verum corpus* while visiting Baden in June and the opera *La clemenza di Tito*, while in Prague. In September, he completes his opera *The Magic Flute*. He also has time to write, among other things, his *Clarinet Concerto in A* and his final work, his magnificent *Requiem*	*The Observer* newspaper begins publication in London and the guillotine is used for the first time in France

02

The Story of Mozart: The Cast List

Major roles

Mozart: *the male lead*

Although his full name was Johannes Chrysostomus Wolfgangus Theophilus Mozart, we're going to call him simply Mozart. If it helps to picture him in your mind as Tom Hulce, who played the lead in the film *Amadeus*, then all well and good. To be fair, though, we hope this story of his life will prove to you that Mozart was a lot

nicer than the film version makes him out to have been.

Leopold: *the father*

A small-time composer in his own right, he is 37 years old when our story begins. He quickly realizes his son's potential – not just as a composer, but also as a pension. Just to be safe in his old age, his daughter also has a huge musical talent that he puts to good use as well.

Colloredo: *the boss*

Full kennel name: The Archbishop Hieronymus, Count Colloredo of Salzburg. (You can see why we're calling him just "Colloredo".) Both a prince and an archbishop, he became the Mozarts' boss when the boy was just 16. He generally gets a bad press, but, as you will see, he does have redeeming features.

Nannerl: *the sister*

Four and a half years older than Mozart, Nannerl was a very good piano player and used to tour with her younger brother as part of the Amazing Mozart Roadshow, often playing in the same concerts. Mozart wrote her countless letters, many of which still survive today. Nannerl was actually her nickname – her real name was Maria Anna.

Constanze: *the wife*

Mozart married Constanze when he was 26, having, some years previously, been smitten by her sister, Aloysia. Constanze's family was not particularly well-off and Leopold did his best to put Mozart off the idea. They seemed to make a very good couple.

Minor roles

Maria Anna: *the mother*

We've put Maria Anna Mozart under "minor roles" because, although he loved her dearly, most of Mozart's correspondence and dealings were with his father. She died while on tour with her son, when Mozart was 22.

Da Ponte: *the lyricist*

Lorenzo Da Ponte wrote the words for Mozart's three biggest opera hits, *The Marriage of Figaro*, *Don Giovanni* and *Così fan tutte*. He was quite a character in his time and scandal of one sort or another was never far away from him. He was much sought after as a lyricist by other composers, too.

Haydn: *the composer*

A nice little cameo role for the composer Haydn. A big friend of Mozart, he was already 24 when our

hero was born and yet lived a full 18 years after Mozart died.

Leutgeb: *the horn player*

He might just as easily be labelled the "cheese shopkeeper" because that was his day job. Leutgeb was a close pal of Mozart to the end. The great man wrote some of classical music's best-loved horn concertos for the cheese shopkeeper. He must have put in quite some hours of practice when he wasn't in the shop because the concertos are written for a very good player.

Puchberg: *the mason*

He could also be called the "money lender". Mozart met Puchberg late in his life, when they were both members of the same masonic lodge. Despite lending Mozart some £30,000 in today's money, it wasn't enough to prevent him from dying in poverty.

Salieri: *a rival composer*

We're calling him "a rival" not "the rival" because Salieri is not quite the baddie that popular mythology has made him out to be. Yes, he was in competition with Mozart on a number of occasions but no, he almost certainly didn't bump him off. Despite history telling a different story, during their lifetimes, Salieri was often more popular than Mozart.

Stadler: *the clarinet player*

The man for whom Mozart wrote much of his clarinet music, including the stunning *Clarinet Concerto*.

Various extras

Arco

Count Arco gains his place in history as "the man who kicked Mozart up the backside", which he did when Colloredo sacked Mozart in 1781.

J.C. Bach

Johann Christian was Johann Sebastian's son. He became friendly with Mozart when they both spent time in London.

Beethoven

Beethoven, only an extra? Well, they met only fleetingly, if indeed at all, and Beethoven was only 22 when Mozart died. So only a walk-on part for Beethoven in this particular *Friendly Guide*.

Galitzin

Prince Dmitry Michailovich Galitzin was the
Russian ambassador in Vienna when Mozart was
a boy.

Hagenauer

Leopold's landlord in Salzburg and recipient of
many letters.

Mesmer

The man who gave his name to the verb to
mesmerize, he was a doctor of medicine and friend
to Mozart.

Rauzzini

A countertenor for whom Mozart wrote his
Exsultate, jubilate.

Schrattenbach

Prince Archbishop Schrattenbach was Leopold's
boss in Salzburg. He was eventually succeeded by
Colloredo.

Spitzeder

A friend of Leopold and a tenor in the Salzburg
court choir.

Süssmayr

The man who finished Mozart's last masterpiece, the *Requiem*, following the composer's death. It was probably a thankless task, when you think about it: do it well and you go down in history as "the man who finished Mozart's last masterpiece". Do it badly and it's worse – "the man who ruined Mozart's last masterpiece".

Weiser

A Salzburg town councillor and textile merchant who provided Mozart with lyrics.

21

03

The Boy Genius

When Mozart was born

27 January 1756

It was a chilly January evening in Salzburg. Leopold Mozart, a musician, was pacing the floors of his flat at No. 9, Getreidegasse. His wife, Maria Anna, was in labour and about to give birth to a son. Despite the fact that this was the seventh time she had been through childbirth, Leopold and his wife only had one surviving child, a girl of 4. In those days, sadly, only a small minority of children survived into adulthood. So, bearing in mind the joy a baby's birth inspires today, you can imagine what Leopold and Maria Anna were feeling when,

at around 8 o'clock that evening, Maria Anna gave birth to a baby boy.

Leopold was originally from the town of Augsburg. Mozart's grandfather had been a bookbinder there and, despite the fact that the family had been in Salzburg for nearly 20 years by the time Mozart was born, Leopold still had several connections with Augsburg, both family and business. As a composer, Leopold would be hugely overshadowed by his new son, but as a violinist, he was very well respected. He was working on a violin teaching book, which was to be published by his friend, the Augsburg publisher, Johann Lotter, and the two exchanged letters on the subject. In one letter, written on 9 February 1756, Leopold included some of his other news to Lotter:

Let me tell you, on 27th January, at 8 o'clock, my darling wife gave birth to a boy . . . both baby and mum are doing well. She sends her best wishes to you two.

What's in a name?

The new baby boy was born on 27 January, which, according to the Catholic calendar, is the feast of St John Chrysostom of Constantinople. The very next day, Leopold had Mozart christened in Salzburg Cathedral. His full name was Johannes Chrysostomus Wolfgangus Theophilus Mozart, which was quite a mouthful. You can see why even Mozart himself very rarely used it all.

So where did all those names come from? Well, Chrysostomus was chosen in light of the saint's day, and Wolfgang was a nod to Leopold's father-in-law, Wolfgang Nikolaus. The Greek name Theophilus, meaning "loved by God" in English, also appears in some documents as "Gottlieb", the German version of the same name, "Amadé", the French version, or the more familiar Latin version, "Amadeus".

Wolfgang Amadeus Mozart tends to be the name by which he is known these days, although Mozart himself preferred people to call him by the French version, Wolfgang Amadé Mozart.

What sort of family was Mozart born into?

In 1756 Mozart's dad, Leopold, was 37, his wife 1 year younger and they had daughter who was not yet 5. The daughter was called Maria Anna, after her mother, but, as the family referred to her by her nickname, Nannerl, so shall we. By the time Mozart was born, his mother Maria Anna had given birth to seven children, but only Nannerl and Mozart had survived. This was such a common scenario that families would often give each child the same family name. So, for example, a mother might give birth to six sons and call them all

Johannes, fully expecting that, at best, only one with the name would survive.

Leopold was quite a respected local musician in Salzburg. He had studied law and philosophy at university, which, although it sounds surprising to us today, was actually quite a common route for musicians. The composer Georg Philipp Telemann did the same. At the age of 20, Leopold had become a musician at Salzburg Cathedral, going on to teach violin at the adjoining choir school. In the course of a modest career, he would become a court musician by the time Mozart was 7 years old.

Mozart's mum, Maria Anna, was 36. As was the way at the time, she was very much secondary to her husband in all things to do with the family. She was not as well-educated – some say she was barely literate – but rather saw it as her duty in life to see to Leopold's every need. She rarely made decisions about family matters.

Nannerl was the fourth of the seven children, but the first to survive beyond infancy. Mozart himself was number seven. By the time Mozart was born, Nannerl was already showing signs of being a musical prodigy. Such was the role of women at that time, though, that despite her obvious gifts, Leopold would devote much more energy into nurturing his son's talents than those of his daughter. A rather stark example of Mozart's advanced status in the pecking order can be seen if you flash forward to "The smallpox incident" on page 53, which occurred when Mozart was 11 years old.

Salzburg then and now

Today, the town of Salzburg clings close to Austria's border with Germany. A picturesque tourist town, its setting beneath the craggy mountains and glacial lakes of the Salzkammergut region makes it a very attractive place for visitors. They come to take the von Trapp Family Tour – the clan made famous by the film *The Sound of Music* lived here in the early days of the Nazis. They come to take in the invigorating mountain air and sample the waters of the nearby spa town of Bad Ischl. And they come for the glorious art and architecture: the Rembrandts and Caravaggios in the Residenzgalerie, the marble façade of the Dom and the gothic delights of the Franziskanerkirche. But more than any of those things, these days, they come to visit the birthplace of probably the world's favourite composer – Wolfgang Amadeus Mozart.

When Mozart was born, Salzburg was a part of the Holy Roman Empire of German Nations, to give it its full title. It was ruled by a prince archbishop, a man who, as his title would suggest, was both a prince and an archbishop. In 1756, the prince

archbishop was called Schrattenbach. He died when Mozart was 15 years old and was replaced by a new prince archbishop called Colloredo. The prince archbishop was the most important man in Salzburg. As well as governing and ruling the area, the prince archbishop's court was the chief musical employer in town. By the time Mozart was born, Leopold already worked for Prince Archbishop Schrattenbach, so you could say that Mozart was born into musical service.

The Holy Roman Empire at that time included almost all the German-speaking countries from the North Sea and the Baltic Sea across to the Alps, as well as what is now Belgium and Luxembourg plus Moravia and Bohemia. The ruling family of the Holy Roman Empire was the house of Habsburg.

Baby Mozart

Despite the fact that his is one of the most researched and documented lives of any of the great composers, precious little is known about Mozart before the age of 5. The pages of numerous biographies remain blank between his second day and his fifth birthday. So, as events over these 5 years fly by – the Seven Years' War, Monroe being elected president of the United States, George III becoming king of England – Mozart's life remains a mystery.

There are two things we do know, though: first, that someone as devoted to his son's musical education as Leopold would almost certainly have started to impart his musical knowledge already; and, second, that at the age of just 3, according to Nannerl, he spent a lot of time at the keyboard, picking out small chords. He was always doing this, she said, and would beam with pride when his embryonic music making sounded good.

When Mozart was five

To be absolutely accurate, Mozart was actually still just 4 years old when he learnt to play his first ever piece of music. Only 3 days before his fifth birthday, Leopold had written out the piece, a scherzo by the Viennese composer, Wagenseil, into Nannerl's notebook for her to practise. At around 9 o'clock in the evening, on 26 January 1761, Mozart opened the notebook and sat down at the keyboard. Just half an hour later, he had learnt to play the piece. Leopold must have been over the moon, but, nevertheless, seems to have calmly noted the moment down, for posterity, using Mozart's nickname:

Wolfgangerl mastered the minuet and trio the day before his fifth birthday, in just thirty minutes, at 9.30 pm, January 26th, 1761.

29

Before the year was out, and no doubt buoyed by his son's daily progress, Leopold felt confident to let the boy play piano in public, at the University of Salzburg. This must have been a bitter-sweet moment for Leopold, who had studied at the university, but had never finished the course.

04

On the Road

When Mozart was six

In some ways, 1762 is a tricky year for us to get our heads around, now. It wasn't the most momentous 12 months in the world's calendar. Rousseau wrote his *Social Contract*, Tzarina Elizabeth of Russia died, to be succeeded first by Peter III and then, upon his assassination, by Catherine II. While the artist George Stubbs was painting "mares and foals", Gluck was premiering his opera, *Orpheus and Eurydice* in Vienna; and Beau Nash "dandied" one final time, before shuffling off his mortal coil.

For Mozart, the year was going to contain an important taste of things to come: 1762 was

significant for him because it was when he was introduced to the art of travel. He undertook three mini-tours across the year, none of them very long in itself, but when taken as a whole, they would have given Mozart – and to be fair, Leopold – some idea of what lay in store for them. In January, they travelled to Munich – a place Mozart would come to know fairly well – where both Nannerl and Mozart were invited to play for Elector Maximilian Joseph.

In October the same year, Leopold hauled both children off to Vienna. Just as it is today, this great city was the beating heart of music in the Austrian lands. Once again, the youngsters were noticed by the powers that be and asked to play at the Viennese court, which they did on 13 October.

Marry Antoinette?

Many stories are told of the young Mozart, but none so illustrates his precociousness as that of his meeting with the ill-fated Marie Antoinette.

It's said that, upon being presented to a then 7-year-old future queen, Mozart – himself a year younger – promptly announced to her that he would, one day, marry her.

The year 1762 was also important for another real first for Mozart: for the first but by no means the last time in his life, he became ill. He was treated by a Doctor von Bernhard, for whom he would later play a concert in thanks, and recovered fairly quickly.

Nevertheless, any illness must have been a worry for Leopold, considering that Mozart and Nannerl were the only two of his seven children to survive.

Ill Divo

Mozart was a sickly child. His first illness, in 1762, was erythema nodosum. Symptoms include painful bruises on the shins and sometimes on other parts of the body. As well as skin lesions, sufferers also have to put up with flu-like symptoms.

His second major illness, the following year, was rheumatic fever, an inflammatory disease that may develop after an infection with Streptococcus *bacteria. Symptoms can include fever, joint pain, joint swelling and a skin rash. These days, it is treated with anti-inflammatory drugs and antibiotics, none of which was available in Mozart's time.*

In December, the family travelled to Pressburg, now known as Bratislava. They returned to their home in Salzburg, some 20 days later, again via Vienna. Even when they got back, Mozart was still ill and bed-bound with rheumatic fever. Mozart's dress rehearsal for his main youthful travels suggested all was not going to be plain sailing when they finally did decide to take to the road for any length of time.

But when would they decide it was a good time to travel? Despite things not having gone terribly well, Leopold surprisingly decided that the time was . . . right now.

What an amazing period this must have been for Mozart. He was just 7 years old and about to set out on a tour of Europe. What he did not know was that by the time he saw Salzburg again, he would be 10. He was about to spend 3 years on the road playing to dukes and barons, emperors and empresses, and kings and queens. At an age when most of us have barely experienced a 1-night sleepover at a school friend's house, Mozart was about to embark on a tour that would take in 17 cities in seven different countries. Now and again, Leopold wrote home to his landlord, with the odd snippet of news about their exploits.

The family set out in the early summer of 1763 and visited Wasserburg on their way to Munich, from where Leopold wrote that Mozart had tried playing the organ. Although he was an accomplished keyboard player, the organ would have been a totally different ball game – mainly because of the intimidating board of pedals at ground level, arranged as an oversized keyboard for the feet. No sooner had Leopold briefly explained what they did, than Mozart was off, playing as if he had been practising for many months. Leopold wrote:

Everyone was amazed. It's another gift from God – the type many people are bestowed with only after hard work.

Leopold and the family were travelling in their own coach and with their own servant, whose name was Sebastian Winter. Just as Mozart himself would do when he was older, Leopold thought it necessary to appear to be on the same level as the people they were visiting. As a result, their luggage was packed full of fine clothes, which Leopold was careful to use sparingly. The mini-tour to Vienna in 1762 had allowed Leopold to stash away the equivalent of 2 years' salary in his Salzburg bank account, so they would be able to survive in relative comfort for quite some time. They arrived in Munich in June and gave four concerts, probably with Mozart and Nannerl playing together in all of them. One of the concerts was on the evening of 13 June 1763. It lasted from 8 o'clock until 11 o'clock. It was hard graft for the two youngsters, but this sort of work rate would stay with Mozart throughout his life.

The family left Munich on 22 June, with the children probably already exhausted, and moved on to Augsburg, Leopold's old stamping ground and still a place where he had family connections. They had been away from home for only 1 month or so of their 3-year grand tour and already Mozart was showing signs of stress. Leopold wrote a letter to his landlord, saying that Mozart woke up several times in the night, homesick and crying. He reeled off a list of names of people in Salzburg whom he was missing. After three concerts in Augsburg, it was on

to Frankfurt and a reminder from Leopold, in case anyone could forget, that this was very much a duo tour, with Mozart and Nannerl getting equal billing:

Frankfort, August 20th, 1763.
We played a concert on the 18th which was great.
Everyone was amazed. Thank God, we are healthy and, wherever we go, much admired. As for little Wolfgangerl, he's astonishingly happy, but also naughty. Little Nannerl is no longer in his shadow, and she now plays with such skill that the world talks of her and marvels at her.

In the first of many "command performances", the father of the German poet and thinker, Johann Wolfgang von Goethe, invited the two prodigies to perform for him, paying Leopold four gulden and seven kreuzers for the privilege.

By September 1763 they had reached Koblenz, from where Leopold wrote, almost incredulously, to his landlord:

We mix only with aristocrats and other distinguished folk . . . honest!

From here, the Magical Mozart Mystery Tour moved on via Brussels to Paris. During Mozart's life, the French capital was, as it has so often been in history, one of the important centres of musical excellence. In much the same way as the pop stars of today will want to "crack America", so classical musicians, and composers in particular, would feel the need to conquer Paris, if only for their personal pride.

Mozart arrived in Paris on 18 November. He and his family would end up staying there for 5 months. To prove that the boast that Leopold made in his letter from Koblenz was in fact true, the family was allowed to lodge on the Rue St Antoine, in the home of Count Maximilian Emanuel Franz von Eyck, and, on 1 January 1764, they gave a concert for Louis XV. Indeed, on one particular occasion, when Mozart was dining with the queen, it's said that he stood by her, kissing her hand while she fed him morsels of food. The Mozarts' reputation preceded them and they were feted by the nobility wherever they went.

If you believe the television adverts for Kronenbourg lager, then 1664 was a very bad year for composing. One hundred years later, though, the signs were much better. It was in Paris in 1764 that a momentous event for classical music occurred. A violin sonata was published, in five movements: the first was quick; the second slow; two minuets and then a final fast movement followed. An 8-year-old Mozart had moved from performer to composer. This was his first published music, his Opus 1.

Fresh from this triumph, on 27 April, the family battle bus moved on to London. If you visit London, you will find three plaques showing where Mozart stayed. The first is at 19 Cecil Court, in Leicester Square, where the family first stayed above what was then a barbershop, but since became, fittingly, a music shop. They then moved to 20 Frith Street in the heart of Soho. In those days it was called Thrift Street, and the family lodged with a Mr Thomas Williamson, a corset maker. There is a blue plaque on the wall of the house now, which is very close to another building with enormous musical heritage: Ronnie Scott's Jazz Club.

Leopold, who was shrewd not only in the exhibiting of his little geniuses, but also in their marketing, displayed posters to attract the right sort of audience to their concerts. Some of these advertisements were addressed to members of the "Nobility and Gentry". Others, such as the one below,

For the benefit of Master MOZART of 8 years, and Miss MOZART, of 12 years of age, prodigies of Nature, before their Departure from England, which will be in six Weeks Time, THERE will be performed, at the End of this Month, or the Beginning of April next, a Concert of Vocal and Instrumental MUSIC. Tickets at Half a Guinea Each. Tickets to be had of Mr Mozart, at Mr Williamson's in Thrift Street, Soho.

seem to somehow have the feel of a freak show, as if Leopold were promoting a travelling circus act.

The marketing obviously worked. They were received by George III himself and gave many concerts. Everyone who was anyone, from noblemen to royalty, was enchanted by Mozart, the boy wonder. Leopold revelled in all the attention and was no doubt also thankful for the hard cash his offspring were generating:

The King presented him with music by Wagenseil, Bach, Abel and Handel, and he played them all at first sight. He played the King's own organ so well that people said his organ playing was better than his piano playing. Next, he accompanied the Queen in a song, and a flute player in a flute and piano piece.

Leopold was also keen to point out that Mozart was learning lots from his time on the road:

In short, his knowledge when he left home is but a shadow of his knowledge now. It's beyond belief.

So, Mozart – and probably his sister – were, to some degree, showcase prodigies, but they were also receiving a musical education, at first hand, in the seminal arenas of music history. This would serve Mozart in particularly good stead when he was

older. On occasions, Leopold gets a bad press for the way in which he exploited his children's talent and, in truth, we're not convinced that he always had his young son's best interests at heart. However, to be fair to him, Mozart would simply have not been the composer he became without the first-hand grasp of the music of the late 18th century's leading composers that was afforded to him through his journeys. Composers did travel in those days, if they were lucky, but generally, they tended not to set out on the road until much later on in life, if at all. Mozart had been to the important musical centres of Europe by the time he was 10 years old. He was young enough to have the opportunity to go back to most of them again.

Life in inner-city Soho obviously did not suit Leopold's constitution and he became unwell. He decided to move the family out to a place where the air was cleaner and there were green fields. It's a measure of how much bigger the city of London is now compared to the 18th century, because it was Chelsea that fitted the bill. They stayed at 180 Ebury Street, as a plaque on the wall of the house still bears testament. They arrived on 6 August and, before they left in September, Mozart had passed an important milestone: he had written his first symphony.

By no means do musical experts these days consider Mozart's *Symphony No. 1* to be a mature work, but

it is, nevertheless, a symphony. It's very easy to forget just how young Mozart was and, right through our *Friendly Guide*, we have to keep stopping to remind ourselves of his age at various key points. This is one of them. He was, let's not forget, still only 8 years old.

One reason that London was the scene of this important landmark might be the fact that the city was at that time home to a member of the Bach clan. Johann Christian Bach was the famous Johann Sebastian Bach's son. He had arrived in England in 1762 at the age of 27 and had never gone back home. His first opera in the capital, *Orione*, so impressed the powers that be that he was immediately appointed Master of Music to Queen Charlotte. J.C. Bach was introduced to Mozart when he arrived and the two soon became friendly. As Leopold mentioned in passing in a letter home:

Mozart sends his best wishes – from the piano stool, where he is, as I write, playing through Kapellmeister [JC] Bach's trio.

J.C. Bach went on to write 90 symphonies and no doubt had some hand in persuading the flamboyant 8-year-old Mozart to dive in himself. A musical footnote here: although J.C. Bach was prolific when it came to penning symphonies, it was his older brother C.P.E. Bach who wrote what

would later be considered important examples of the genre.

On 27 January 1765, Mozart celebrated his ninth birthday. Ever keen to do the right thing in each "territory" in which they found themselves, Leopold had Mozart dedicate three piano sonatas to Queen Charlotte. Across the several months of their stay in London, Leopold felt his hard work had been repaid more than in any other place:

At every court, it's true, we've been received astonishingly graciously but what we've experienced in England outshines the rest.

As the business brain behind the entire Mozart enterprise, it would have been Leopold who set the two children to work in 1765, playing concerts in order to recoup some of the money spent on his medical bills. Having played a concert in February, Mozart and Nannerl were booked in at a London pub called the Swan and Harp for an entire week of concerts. The pair played from noon until 3 o'clock every day for 7 days in order to make up for lost time. When they finally left London, they must have been shattered. They travelled back through the Kent countryside, stopping off in Canterbury and Dover. Leopold wrote that Mozart was, despite his illness and his tiredness, dreaming of a new work for "young people":

His mind is now occupied with an opera, which he's hoping to put on back in Salzburg, with only young people. I've been helping him work out which young folk he might sign up for his orchestra.

On 1 August, the family arrived in Calais, where their coach was waiting for them, ready to whisk them off to Lille. In Lille, both father and son were ill, Leopold with angina. By the time they reached The Hague, in September, Nannerl made the list of invalids three out of four, coming down with intestinal typhoid. As a result, a recovering Mozart was forced to play his first ever solo concert. All went well. He also published six violin sonatas. By now, and no doubt with some encouragement from his father, he had already taught himself to play the instrument.

In 1766, far from winding down the tour as they made their way back home, the schedule became ever more punishing. By the time the first signs of summer had arrived in May, Mozart had already played in Utrecht, Amsterdam, Antwerp and Brussels. Leopold's experiences on tour had been a revelation to him. Back in Salzburg, he was a mere public servant, paid – not a massive amount – to provide music on demand. On the road, the family were received by royalty and treated almost as equals. Just as would be the case for Mozart some years later, Leopold had no burning desire to return to the status quo. So, on 10 May, they

revisited Paris. They stayed there for 2 leisurely months and, concerts and receptions aside, behaved like tourists.

They had a portrait painted with Mozart seated at the harpsichord at the Prince de Conti's tea party. To be fair, the painting was more of the tea party than it was of Mozart, the Prince de Conti no doubt using Mozart as much as a trophy as a musician. In fact, the canvas is mainly a picture of the room. Two-thirds of it is a huge picture of the décor, behind the guests. Then, of the third that depicts the party, Mozart and his harpsichord occupy but a third again. Just like a cab driver boasting about whom he has had in the back of his cab, De Conti was saying "I have a beautiful house, I had a great party, and, look, I had that Mozart playing for me, too!" The picture is also another useful way of reminding ourselves of the scale of Mozart's achievements. In the midst of this genteel collection of guests, Mozart is a bizarre, tiny figure, looking as if he has had to be helped up on to his chair.

Given the warm welcome that the Mozart family received at numerous high-profile events such as the Prince de Conti's tea party, it's hardly surprising that Leopold didn't rush home. He was reluctant to leave Paris, but when the time came, the family travelled to Dijon for another concert, where the 10-year-old Mozart, who was almost certainly an able boy soprano, sang one of his own arias. From there, it was on, via Switzerland, to Munich.

They had first visited Munich at the start of their tour, but that was now 3 years ago. It was then that Mozart had played the organ for the first time, dazzling his audience in the process. This time, arriving on 9 November and staying for just 3 weeks, they probably made an even bigger impression than the last. Mozart was still a boy wonder, but now had 3 years more experience – and 3 years, in Mozart terms, was eons. Those people who saw him play would have been faced with the double-whammy of him still being a slip of a child (because Mozart was always short, even for his age) and of now being an even more accomplished, more spectacular artist than before. The audiences must have loved it. He was immediately invited to play at court, which he did: first on his own then, after a short illness, with Nannerl. What a time they must have had. What euphoria they must have felt. And how hard must reality have bitten when they finally, on 29 November, hit Salzburg. Mozart's 3 years on the road had come to an end.

The Mozart show: life on the road

When he was between the ages of 7 and 10, Mozart was more or less permanently on the road. His amazing talents – and, to a lesser extent, his sister's too – ensured that, wherever they went, they were treated like kings. But to arrive in each new town, fresh and perfectly presented, took some doing.

At every major destination, Leopold would almost immediately offer to play a concert, which would draw out the "music lovers" and important noblemen of the town, keen to hear the phenomenon that all Europe was talking about. Usually, Leopold was carrying a letter of introduction with him, either from Salzburg or from a previous town. Where they could not compose pieces in time, pre-existing pieces were dedicated to the most important person in a territory. Usually, it paid off, with gifts such as snuffboxes, gold watches and, of course, cash being bestowed on the great young marvel. The six sonatas dedicated to Queen Charlotte elicited a present of 50 guineas.

The prodigy

The three questions we're asking and answering in this section are:

1 Was Mozart just like any other prodigy?
2 Was he just a unique talent that was spotted early and nurtured?
3 What effect did periods such as his 3 years on the road from the age of 7 have on him?

46

Later on in life, when Leopold was at home and Mozart was on the road alone, Leopold tutored him in how to seek out the most important nobleman in the town; how to find out their musical tastes and compose accordingly; and, most interestingly of all, how to manage his wardrobe so that he did not waste his best clothes on the wrong people.

The family carried with them the correct clothes for the correct events. Leopold refers to the act of "producing themselves" – the act of making sure they gave off the right impression at the right time. As expensive as it was, this meant buying a new wardrobe to suit the territory. So when they were in England, they had no choice but to buy English clothes. Leopold wrote home:

> *Imagine how my wife, my little girl, myself and big Wolfgang look in English clothes!*

Well, the answers, in our opinion, are:

1 "No."
2 "Yes and no."
3 "Well, how long have you got?"

Let's start at the beginning.

Was he just like any other prodigy? Well, quite clearly, no, he was not. His was not just a big talent, it was that of a *genius*. His father believed he had an

almost "divine" talent, which it was his duty to nurture to its peak. You can see this in the things Mozart was able to do. Many children can develop an affinity with a certain instrument or discipline, but Mozart could kick-start those talents himself. When he first stepped up onto the organ, he could play the pedal board, consummately, even though nobody had previously taught him how to do it. Just because someone is a proficient pianist, it does not automatically follow that they will make a good organist – ask any professional pianist or organist, if you don't believe us. Mastering the pedals on an organ can take a lot of time: a pianist is taught to coordinate his left and his right hands to play both as one and as two. Taming a pedal board requires a whole new set of skills. Mozart also taught himself violin. Admittedly, his father was one of the greatest violin teachers of his day, but nevertheless, he was able to sow the fiddling seed and grow it by himself.

Was Mozart just a unique talent that was spotted early and nurtured, just like any other? Yes and no. Mozart toured, or rather *was toured*, relentlessly. This must have been as hard on him as it would be on any youngster, but it gave him an invaluable insight into all manner of different composers and their musical styles. The value of this should not be underestimated. The combination of his unique talent – and it was like no other, before or since – and what Leopold did to it, produced one of the greatest musical minds ever to have graced the planet.

And what effect did periods such as his 3 years on the road from the age of 7 have on him? Well, as we said earlier, how long have you got? The beneficial effects are plain to see: Mozart touched, at first hand, all manner of musical threads and wove them into his own one-off tapestry. His youthful works show him assimilating, copying and mimicking the music and techniques he came across on tour. Gradually, these became absorbed and he began to produce his own statements, works that could only be "fingerprint" Mozart pieces. Sports coaches today would describe the concentrated nurturing of his talents as "hothousing". The great artistic and sporting heroes often make sacrifices during their pursuit of excellence and, in Mozart's case, his success came with its own set of strings attached.

It is true that he knew no different, but being away from other children and almost on his own, save for Nannerl, must have taken its toll on the young boy. We have already heard how he could wake up, crying for Salzburg and the people he knew. What is less well-documented is the fact that Mozart would frequently ask people he had only recently met if they loved him. The meeting with Marie Antoinette may now be related as a vaguely comic event, but it was probably part of a wider trait that suggests he had a number of issues when it came to loving and

being loved. These traits of high self-esteem, or even arrogance, coupled with bouts of self-doubt and an intense need to be loved are common among many high-achieving artistic performers.

It's raining, It's pouring, the young man's . . .

On the many trips he shared with his young son, Leopold must have come to know virtually everything there was to know about him. They were forced, on occasions, to share beds, often leading to one or the other of them getting little or no sleep. Leopold's letters also make a point of noting that the young composer snored. So, next time you are told off for snoring, or dug in the ribs in the middle of the night and asked to quieten down, maybe you could reply that, well, if it's ok for the world's greatest composer to snore, then it's ok for you. Who knows – maybe it's a sign of genius?

The seven-year-old's war

Eventually Mozart shared his father's misgivings about Salzburg. But when he was still a child, simply being away from home, very often without one or other of his parents, would have tangibly affected the young composer. Living out of a suitcase today is stressful enough, but back then it must have been almost mind-boggling. Leaving aside the length and discomfort of the travel, there were many other factors that conspired to make life difficult. Although, as you can see in Chapter 1 of our *Friendly Guide*, Mozart lived through relatively peaceful times, the periods in between wars were not without their hazards.

Travelling exposed you to far more opportunities to catch the seemingly endless round of epidemics that hit Europe at the time, and the Mozarts had their fair share. Finding healthy food was an issue, as was the occasional threat of daylight robbery. Add to this the language barriers and the varying states of accommodation and a less than ideal way of life emerges. True, royal banquets and heroic welcomes were nice, but if we draw up a list of the positives and negatives of the quality of life as an itinerant musician in the 18th century, there is always going to be a large column marked "minus".

Overall, though, Mozart appears to have come out of his childhood tours remarkably intact as a person. Only later, very much later, did his early life on the road appear to take its toll.

When Mozart was eleven

Back in Salzburg, things returned to normal for Leopold. For Mozart himself, there probably was no version of "normal" to return to. He had been only 7 when they left home and had travelled for much of the year leading up to his grand tour, anyway. On the road, when he had woken up with nightmares, fretting for the people back home, the names he

spoke of were almost all adults: Hagenauer, Leopold's landlord; Leutgeb, the horn player; and Spitzeder, the tenor in the Salzburg court choir – all of them friends of Leopold, rather than of Mozart. Apart from his sister, Nannerl, Mozart enjoyed very little company of his own age. The fact that he spent his childhood mixing almost exclusively in adult company is one of the reasons many have suggested he took some of the signs of juvenilia into later life with him. Perhaps it was part of being a highly creative individual, but there is no doubt that Mozart kept a part of himself forever young.

The return home allowed Leopold the chance to show Salzburg how his young Wunderkind had improved. Mozart set to work on a cantata entitled *Die Schuldigkeit des ersten Gebots*. For the words, Mozart looked to a friend of his father's named Anton Weiser, who was a town councillor and textile merchant in Salzburg. He was an influential man, so the arrangement was probably as much down to diplomacy as it was for aesthetic reasons. The aria was performed at the Archbishop Schrattenbach's court on 12 April that year, and, much to Leopold's delight, they received 12 ducats for it. The young Mozart was equally delighted with the golden medal, which was given to him personally.

To be fair to Mozart, he did not have long to find himself a comfortable version of childhood life in Salzburg because, less than 9 months after they had come home, Leopold asked for leave to go back on the road. Schrattenbach agreed and the family set the coordinates for Vienna. Once they arrived, though, they found the city overrun by a smallpox epidemic.

The smallpox incident

It's 1767. Mozart is 11. He and the family are temporarily in Vienna. A smallpox epidemic has hit the city. The house in which they are staying appears to be rather badly affected and several of the landlord's children have gone down with the disease. Leopold is very concerned to protect his biggest asset — Mozart. He frantically searches for new rooms, but can find none big enough to house the whole family — himself, Maria Anna, Nannerl and Mozart. So, thinking more as a cool, calculating concert promoter than as a loving husband and father, Leopold moves out with Mozart, to stay with a friend who can only accommodate two. He leaves Maria Anna and Nannerl back in the infected house to fend for themselves.

Eventually, though, Leopold decided that, as important as Vienna was to Mozart, it was not worth risking the health and wellbeing of his family. All four Mozarts upped sticks and decamped to Bohemia, arriving on 23 October. Almost as soon as they arrived there, Mozart went down with smallpox, although he had almost certainly contracted it in Vienna. On 26 October, in Olomouc (which was then called Olmütz), Leopold called in a Doctor Wolff and Mozart was ordered to rest for at least a couple of months.

By December, Mozart was a lot better and the family moved on to Brno (then known as Brünn) where, just 4 days after Christmas, Mozart was well enough to give a concert with Nannerl in a tavern in the town. Buoyed by his son's improvement, and with news that the Austrian capital was once again rid of the disease, Leopold waited just 10 days into the New Year before setting out to Vienna once more. It took the family a further 10 days travelling to get there and they finally arrived on 20 January 1768. Promisingly, the day they arrived, they were immediately received at court. Maybe this time things would work out?

Smallpox

The facts and figures surrounding smallpox make for very sobering reading. It is an acute contagious disease, which is believed to have originated more than 3000 years ago in India or Egypt. It is one of the most devastating diseases known to mankind. For hundreds of years, it rampaged unchecked across continents.

Smallpox was no respecter of status, with monarchs just as likely as their subjects to succumb to the disease. Among those it claimed were Queen Mary II of England, Emperor Joseph I of Austria, King Luis I of Spain, Tzar Peter II of Russia, Queen Ulrika Elenora of Sweden and King Louis XV of France.

No effective treatment for the disease has ever been developed and 30% of those infected eventually die. Up to

When Mozart was twelve

Dmitry Michailovich Galitzin, or Prince Dmitry
Michailovich Galitzin, to give him his full title, is
not a name that you might instantly bring to mind
when thinking of Mozart. Yet, as happened with a
number of the folk who get their name in our cast
list of extras, he was one of those people whose
contribution, when added to the rest, made a big
difference to our hero.

Born in Abo in what is now Finland, Galitzin was
the Russian Ambassador in Vienna. As such, he
would have organized any number of parties to

*80% of those who survive are marked with deep-pitted scars
(pockmarks). These are most prominent on the face.*

*The statistics from the 18th century, when Mozart was
struck down with smallpox, are terrifying. The disease claimed
the lives of one in ten children born in Sweden and France. It
was even worse in Russia, where one in seven children died.*

*Edward Jenner invented a vaccine in 1798, but 150 years
later there were still an estimated 50 million cases of smallpox
in the world each year. In 1967 there were still 10–15
million cases, but the vaccination programme has worked,
with the last naturally occurring case in Somalia in 1977.
The global eradication of smallpox was certified by a
commission of eminent scientists in December 1979.*

Source: World Health Organization

which the higher echelons of Viennese society were invited. At each event, he would have wanted to provide his guests with entertainment more rich and varied than before. It was no doubt as much with this in mind as with an eye to patronage that he would have wanted the amazing Mozart children at his house.

Mozart and Nannerl were duly invited to perform in his home in March that year and gave a concert together to an audience of Vienna's finest. The concert went well, except for one thing. It was here, at Galitzin's, and from this point on, that rumours began to surface about Mozart "the boy wonder" and, in particular, about the authenticity of his compositions.

During his time in Vienna, Mozart wrote an opera, *La finta semplice*, which translates as "The make-believe idiot". Leopold tried hard to get the work performed, but to no avail. The rumours circulating about Mozart were getting stronger. While some were saying, as they had always done, that Mozart's musicality was nothing short of miraculous, others were beginning to doubt that a miracle of this magnitude could occur. A 12-year-old boy? Writing a fully fledged opera? Well, it couldn't be possible. They believed it must have been the work of Leopold, who was passing off his own compositions as the boy's to make money! But the live performances that astonished crowds when they witnessed them first hand? How could they be faked? Well, obviously some of the reports were just lies, claimed the detractors. But what about the way he could improvise, spectacularly, on themes given to him by members of his audience? And the way he could play virtually any piece from sight? Well, clearly, so the rumourmongers would say, these were pulled off with prearranged stooges, in much the same way as cheap conjurers would do. Leopold was furious at the malicious stories being peddled about him and his son:

These days, people make fun of miracles. They question them. So, you have to put them right.

For a while, Leopold's attempts to demonstrate the music as his son's genius seemed to work:

It was very satisfying – and a personal victory – to hear someone say "Today, for the first time in my life, I have witnessed a miracle!"

Was he winning the battle? Sadly, no. He could not find anywhere willing to premiere Mozart's opera, which would have to wait a good year to be heard. It was eventually performed back home in Salzburg. Leopold even, for a time, suspected that the scurrilous accusations might not be genuine scepticism, but rather the machinations of jealous fellow composers, keen not to be upstaged by a mere boy of 12. He even considered, for a time,

that it might have been the composer Christoph
Willibald von Gluck, plotting against Mozart's
reputation, but there does not appear to be much to
back up this theory. In the end, Leopold decided to
play a waiting game:

*I'll wait til the Emperor gets here, before doing battle.
Mark my words, I will stop at nothing to protect the
reputation of my son . . . Patience! Time will sort
things out.*

As if to show the world that *La finta semplice* was
not merely a flash in the pan, Mozart composed
another opera, *Bastien and Bastienne*. This opera
would get a performance in Vienna – and it would
mesmerize the Viennese in the process.

Franz Mesmer, one of the leading lights of Viennese
society – and, by then, not yet tarnished with his

Doctor Franz Mesmer

*If you've ever heard the word "mesmerized" and wondered
where it came from, you probably never thought it had
anything to do with Mozart. Franz Mesmer was a fully
qualified doctor who lived in Vienna. The year Mozart wrote*
Bastien and Bastienne, *the good doctor married a wealthy
Viennese widow and the two settled down to a very
comfortable life of medicine and the arts. Mesmer had a
complete theatre in his back garden in Vienna and, as a
singer, pianist and cellist, he was often to be found*

"mesmerizing" experiments – invited Leopold to stage Mozart's new opera in his garden theatre, an event that probably took place around October. In addition, across the autumn, Mozart wrote his first complete mass, which was performed in the church of a Viennese orphanage in December. The 12-year-old Mozart was himself the conductor of the premiere. From Leopold's letters, it appears his waiting game was paying off:

Wolfgang's Mass, performed on 7th December . . . with the Imperial family in attendance and Wolfgang himself conducting, has repaired the damage our enemies sought to do by blocking the opera, and has convinced both the court and the public – who turned up in droves – of the malevolence of our rivals!

The mass became known by its venue, *Waisenhausmesse*, which translates as the

entertaining high society at home. Later, in the 1770s, he began to develop his theories on "animal magnetism" as a way of healing, but his methods were not altogether successful. Having demonstrably failed to cure a blind patient, the pianist Maria Theresia von Paradies, he left Vienna for Paris. Interestingly enough, when Mozart came to write his opera Così fan tutte, *he half poked fun at Mesmer by having one of the characters, Despina, disguise herself as a doctor and bring someone back to life with the help of a Mesmer magnet.*

"Orphanage Mass". Cheered considerably by
the emperor's reception and attendance, Leopold led
the clan back home to Salzburg.

When Mozart was thirteen

Little did he know at the outset, but 1769 was
going to prove an important year for Mozart.
He spent virtually the whole time in Salzburg,
which must have felt rather unusual for him. As
a result, his compositions were created almost
exclusively for Archbishop Schrattenbach's court
and for the adjoining university. There was a
Missa brevis, performed at Salzburg's
Kollegienkirche, and a mass for Leopold's
landlord, Hagenauer, although dedicated to him
in his role as "Father Domenicus" Hagenauer.
Hence, the *Domenicus Mass* was performed at
the abbey church of St Peter, Salzburg, on
15 October.

It was in the autumn, on 27 November to be exact,
that Mozart's world changed, quite considerably. He
was given the post of Konzertmeister to the
Salzburg court. Although the role came without
pay, the significance of this opportunity is hard to
overestimate. This was a 13-year-old boy being
given the job as a composer and conductor to the
prince archbishop of one of the major principalities
of the Holy Roman Empire.

Leopold was overjoyed with the appointment, not least because Schrattenbach chose this moment to give Mozart 120 ducats. Leopold knew exactly what Mozart should do with his money, too. Leaving Nannerl at home with her mother, Leopold immediately set about packing bags, firing off letters and, generally, organizing travel plans. Within 2 weeks, he had Mozart ready to go back on the road, this time as a solo performer. They were going to Italy.

On 13 December 1769, the teenage composer and his dad settled down to a good 2 weeks on the road, the rediscovered novelty of coach travel still a source of excitement for Mozart, if not for his father. Mozart wrote home to his mum barely a week into the journey:

I feel so happy on this journey. It's lovely and warm in the carriage, and our driver is a bold chap who drives like the wind whenever the roads allow!

On 17 December, they stopped at Innsbruck, finding time to play at the house of a local nobleman, Count Künigl. From there, it was non-stop travelling in the coach for almost 10 days, until the day after Boxing Day, when they arrived safe and well in Verona. Mozart's Italian Adventure had begun.

Wolfie's on the road again: Mozart in Italy

Before we get on to Italy, a little aside. Although it may look flippant, the term "Wolfie" – so memorably used in the film version of Peter Shaffer's Amadeus *– is, more or less, accurate. Just as Mozart's sister's name, Maria Anna, was transformed into Nannerl – a pretty untranslatable nickname – so Mozart had his name changed by the family too. His was lengthened from Wolfgang to Wolfgangerl – which, although, again, pretty untranslatable, would probably end up coming out something like "Wolfie" in English.*

Although it has shifted across the centuries, the centre of the classical music universe in the 18th century was quite definitely Italy. To be fair, the country had justifiably earned the accolade. Previously, places such as the Netherlands and northern France had laid claim to the title, but, when Mozart was 13, the Italians were definitely the dominant force when it came to composing classical music.

Many of Leopold's letters complain of his boss, Schrattenbach, allowing Italian musicians to dominate the Salzburg court or being too easily overawed by any composer or performer with so much as an Italian name. On one occasion, when there was a vacant position as a violinist in the court orchestra to be filled, Schrattenbach had a fiddler immediately shipped over from Italy, assuming that, as an Italian, he must be better than anything Salzburg had to offer. Leopold, who had fancied the position for one of his pupils, was more than a little smug when the new Italian turned out to be a disaster. The fact that he left under a cloud, leaving a young girl pregnant, was, to be fair, something neither party could have foreseen.

For Leopold, Italy was Mozart's great big hope. The Italians, surely, would recognize Mozart's genius as a performer and, more importantly, his future potential as a composer? Leopold had big plans for Mozart in Italy. At the head of the list was his desire for his son to secure a job in one of the renowned Italian courts.

Mozart spent around 2 weeks in Verona where, among other things, he had his portrait painted – not for himself, but for Pietro Lugiati, who was fairly high up in the local tax office in Verona and, being a bit of a music lover, hosted the Mozarts on a couple of occasions. He was clearly smitten with Mozart's composing and playing and commissioned the artist, Saverio dalla Rosa, to paint his portrait. These days, you might ask to have your photograph taken with a famous performer, but in those days, if you wanted to remind yourself of someone, you had to commission a portrait. Dalla Rosa's picture shows Mozart, just 3 weeks away from his 14th birthday, sitting playing at a harpsichord. He is wearing a red

coat with a white ruff, hands on the keyboard, looking backwards to his right. Due to the relative scarcity of authenticated pictures of Mozart, it is one that has come to adorn numerous Mozart books and mementos. If you visit Salzburg, you'll even find it as the wrapping around the city's most popular tourist chocolate, the Mozartkugel.

When Mozart was fourteen

Mozart gave two concerts in Verona, before moving on to Milan. He and Leopold arrived on 23 January 1770 and settled into the Augustinian monastery of San Marco. The building's beautiful rose window is still popular with tourists today. It looks out on to the Piazza San Marco and if you visit, you will see a plaque on the wall, which reads:

Wolfgang Amadeus Mozart was a guest here of the Augustinian fathers during his first stay in Milan January 23rd – March 15th, 1770.

In Milan, music oozed from every pore of the city. The opera-going public was continually treated to the best composers that Italy had to offer. In terms of concerts, the veteran composer Sammartini was dominant and still revered by the Milanese, having never left the place during his whole life. Sammartini had two main claims to fame. His symphonies were probably the most important in Italy at the time and he was also the teacher of

another great composer, Gluck. By 1770 Gluck had already written *Orfeo ed Euridice*, which had blown the opera world apart with its new sounds. Mozart sampled the opera in Milan "six or seven times" and wrote home to his sister, waxing lyrical about the festivities that started when the opera finished – "a fine sight".

At this stage in his life, many of Mozart's thoughts survive as postscripts to his father's letters. Rather like the "and finally" story on a television news bulletin, they give us a glimpse of Mozart's slightly off-the-wall sense of humour. In an addition to Leopold's note of 10 February 1770, Mozart wrote:

Speak of the Devil and he will appear . . . I kiss Mum's hand, send my sister a smacker of a kiss, and remain the undersigned – guess who? – the undersigned Jack-pudding, Wolfgang in Germany, Amadeo in Italy, De Mozartini.

So, next time you need an icebreaker at a dinner party and somebody mentions Mozart, maybe let slip "Ah, old Jack-pudding" and see where the conversation goes.

After several pleasant evenings eating and entertaining at the house of a local noble, Count von Firmian, the entourage moved on to Florence. Leopold wrote home to his wife and wearily

explained that Mozart had wowed the local nobility yet again:

Count von Firmian was extremely enthused by little Wolfgang's talent . . . It would be too tiresome to tell you in detail what proof of his genius Wolfgang gave while Sammartini and guests looked on, all of them astonished. You know only too well what happens on these occasions – you've seen it often enough.

They spent just under 2 weeks in Florence, where Mozart played for Grand Duke Leopold, who later became emperor. Slightly the worse for wear from a heavy cold, Mozart arrived in Rome on 11 April, just in time for Easter.

With the Vatican at the heart of Rome, Easter was, as you might imagine, a grand affair. For Mozart, the city was captivating. He was overawed by St Peter's, desperately wishing his sister could have been with them. In line with tradition, he kissed the foot of St Peter, but, being rather short, had to be lifted up to reach. He drew pictures of St Luke, St Paul and St Peter in his notebook. But, perhaps unsurprisingly, the greatest impression on the 14 year old's memory was left by a piece of music.

While he was in St Peter's, Mozart heard an Easter performance of the *Miserere*, which would have been sung on the Thursday, Friday and Saturday of Holy Week. He was immediately enchanted by its

high, sweeping choral parts. The piece had been written for the Sistine Chapel choir over a century and a half earlier by the priest and composer, Gregorio Allegri.

It is easy for us to forget now, in the age of printed music on demand, that back then, musical manuscripts were not only far harder to come by, but also far easier to abuse. Composers tended to guard their music jealously, in the absence of copyright laws to prevent other composers from copying it, stealing it or, worse still, passing it off as their own. One way to protect music was to not write it down at all, but to pass it on orally, from generation to generation. If the music manuscripts for Allegri's *Miserere* did exist, they were only circulated among the members of the Sistine Chapel choir.

Mozart, though, was so taken by the piece that he returned home to his lodgings – where he was currently sharing a bed with his father and, hence getting no sleep at all – and wrote the entire piece out from memory, part perfect. He went back to St Peter's to hear the work again, probably the same week, to check his written-out score with the sung version.

Mozart's Italian year continued with sightseeing in Naples, before he headed back to Rome to receive an honour from the Pope. He was awarded the Order of the Golden Spur in a ceremony which saw

him dressed in full honours regalia. In late July, the father and son team arrived in Bologna. Leopold had a bit of an accident and they were forced to rest up at the estate of Count Pallavicini, just outside the city. Despite the temporary hold up, Mozart's reputation was moving on in leaps and bounds. The accolades continued in Bologna: he was admitted to the prestigious Accademia Filarmonica and given a diploma. No doubt the ailing Leopold would rather have had money and commissions than honours and diplomas. As he would later say: "Nice words, tributes and cries of bravo will pay neither the postman nor the landlord!"

When they arrived back in Milan, Leopold must have been heartened to see Mozart starting work on a commission for an opera. He put so much effort into it that it even affected his letter writing:

I can't write much, because writing so many parts of the opera has made my fingers painful.

It was the tradition at the time to write the recitatives first. These are the parts of an opera that are very wordy, often advance the plot and usually come before or after the actual arias. The arias themselves were often written a lot closer to the time of the premiere. This allowed the composer to write for the actual singers taking part in the first night of the opera. It was also another way in which a composer could guard their music from their competitors.

The closer to an opening night that you revealed your "hit" songs, the less chance there was that someone might pinch them. Mozart started work on his recitatives in the October of 1770, much to the general scepticism of many in the Milan opera company. The doubters knew that he was prodigious, but giving him the job of writing an Italian opera for a proper, professional company? Surely not? They were soon singing from a different hymn sheet, though. As Leopold wrote home when the company came together to practise the new work:

Since the first rehearsal night, all these people have been silenced, and they left without a word.

The opening night on 26 December at the Teatro Regio Ducal, with Mozart himself conducting, was an even better experience:

Two things happened, unheard of in Milan. One of the soprano's arias was repeated! And, after almost every aria, there was amazing applause and shouts of "Long live the Little Maestro!"

The opera was called *Mitridate, rè di Ponto*. It is now overshadowed by Mozart's later operatic work and as a result is rarely performed today.

The taste of success continued into the new year of 1771. Just days before his 15th birthday, Mozart received yet more honours, this time a diploma

from the Accademia Filarmonica of Verona. Italy, it seemed, was taken with Mozart.

When Mozart was fifteen

It was 1771 and another Italian "campaign" was coming to an end for the Mozarts. February saw them in Venice, sampling the carnival atmosphere and, of course, giving concerts. While they were there, Mozart found that the success of his opera *Mitridate, rè di Ponto* was starting to bear fruits. He received a commission for a new opera, which was also to be staged in Milan. The family returned home to Salzburg on something of a high on 28 March, having been away for 15 months. Just 4 months later, they needed to start packing again. They arrived in Milan on 21 August after a hot and sticky journey. Mozart wrote to his sister:

The dust stifled us like mad – if we'd not been careful, we could have choked on it. It's not rained in Milan for a MONTH (so they say) and, despite it spitting a little yesterday, the sun's out again and it's pretty hot . . . I'm huffing and puffing with the heat – I think I might burst!

He was happy with the rooms where they were staying though:

There's a fiddler above us, another fiddler beneath us, a singing teacher giving lessons next door and opposite us

an oboe player. It's great for composing – it gives you lots of ideas!

True enough, when he was presented with a libretto for a new opera, *Ascanio in Alba*, he was brimful of ideas and the rehearsals began within a month. The premiere took place at the Teatro Regio Ducal, by way of a celebration of the marriage of Princess Beatrice to Archduke Ferdinand. The archduke was clearly impressed and, so the story goes, was minded to offer Mozart a position. This was the closest Mozart had come so far to Leopold's "promised land" of a steady job.

Sadly, Princess Beatrice was not in favour of the idea and, when Mozart and Leopold returned to Salzburg on 15 December, Mozart was in his usual state – feted, yet jobless. One day later, though, their world was turned on its head. Schrattenbach, their prince, their archbishop and, more importantly their employer, died.

When Mozart was sixteen

New Year 1773 saw Mozart focused very much on Salzburg. A new prince archbishop meant a completely new start for the Mozarts. Nothing could be taken for granted – relationships needed to be forged, positions needed to be maintained. For the enthronement ceremony, Mozart set to music

words by the grand old man of the libretto world, the 74-year-old poet, Metastasio. It wasn't an opera, it wasn't an oratorio, it was a "dramatic serenade". And it was successfully performed at the enthronement on 1 May that year. Again, although it was undoubtedly of good quality and certainly important at that moment, it has not survived the test of time to claim a place in the general repertoire.

The new prince archbishop was called Colloredo. In the summer of 1772, he settled a few nerves in the Mozart household by confirming the 16-year-old composer in his job of Konzertmeister, on a yearly salary of 150 gulden. When their new boss granted them another leave of absence to go to Italy again, in October, the Mozarts could be forgiven for thinking that it was going to be business as usual, as far as the prince archbishop was concerned. It turned out that they could not have been more wrong.

Mozart and Leopold left for Milan in late October, arriving in early November. Their reason for travelling – apart from any excuse to leave Salzburg on Mozart's part – was to start rehearsals for the new opera, commissioned the previous year. It was to be called *Lucio Silla* and it was premiered on Boxing Day. It did very well initially, notching up 20 performances in its first month.

Opera to go

Our friendly guide to ordering your opera:

Opera seria: *like espresso: a serious, strong opera.*

Opera buffa: *more of a cappuccino: frothy, light and with lots of sweetness sprinkled on top.*

Singspiel: *a bit of a mocha, neither one thing nor the other: a play with music. A bit like a musical: everyone stops for a song, then carries on.*

Incidentally, the person singing the lead role in *Lucio Silla* was a castrato in his late twenties called Venanzio Rauzzini. Mozart was particularly impressed with him and wrote him a three-movement motet, *Exsultate, jubilate*, which these days is generally sung by female sopranos. The last movement was a bit of a show-off, for both composer and performer. Mozart gave himself the task of setting just one word, "Alleluia", for the entire movement. With its fast-paced and incredibly catchy vocal line, Rauzzini must have loved it. It was first heard on 17 January, 1773 at Milan's Theatine Church. *Exsultate, jubilate* is an important piece for Mozart and it is one of the few pieces he wrote before adulthood that has remained among his most popular works.

When Mozart was seventeen

Today, they say that moving house is the one of the most stressful things a person can experience, second only to divorce. For the close-knit Mozart family, experience number one would never happen, but experience number two took place in the March of 1773.

To be fair, they weren't moving far – from the Getreidegasse, close to the south bank of the River Salzer, just across the bridge to Hannibal-Platz on the north bank. If you are in Salzburg searching for the new house, don't go looking for Hannibal-Platz because you'll never find it: the street now goes by the name of Makartplatz. Mozart's house was at No. 8. It is now called the Dance Master's House, although most of the building was destroyed by bombing by the allied forces in October 1944. It was renovated in 1995 and today is often used for concerts in the tourist season.

The new pad was not enough to keep the Mozarts home for long and by July, Mozart and his father were on the road again to Vienna. As usual, Mozart was seeking gainful employment. At first, things looked good when he was granted an audience with the empress and they gave concerts at society houses, including Dr Mesmer's again. They were invited to a special feast day dinner, where

Mozart once more wowed his audience, this time with his virtuosity on the violin. But it was the same old story; everything seemed to come to nothing and on 27 September, they resurfaced in Salzburg with no job offer to consider.

When Mozart was eighteen

Amazingly enough, the Mozart family resisted the urge to travel for almost the whole of 1774. Then again, perhaps it wasn't so surprising considering that for the first 21 months of Colloredo's reign, Mozart was only at home for around 11 of them. So, Mozart spent the year busying himself with a variety of compositions, including masses for the archbishop, which were written specifically to his particular tastes.

All this time, though, Mozart's musical voice was maturing. With every piece, it was not only easier to identify the hand of the composer, but also each work grew in accomplishment. Milestones such as his *Symphony No. 29*, which was finished on 6 April this year, show his music truly coming of age. Also in 1774, he wrote the *Bassoon Concerto*. In this work, Mozart gave his bassoon soloist a real run out on the instrument, with fast, florid passages that are still something of a trial today, never mind on the considerably more unwieldy instrument of the 1770s.

With his operas, too, he was moving on in leaps and bounds, sounding ever more profound notes. When a commission came that year from Munich, the resulting work, *La finta giardiniera* (an opera buffa) is yards more accomplished than his previous comic work, *La finta semplice*. Of course, it also provided Mozart with a reason to leave Salzburg. He and his father arrived in Munich on 6 December that year to attend rehearsals of the new opera.

While he was there, Mozart acquired a bad case of toothache, as he told his sister, Nannerl, in a postscript to Leopold's letter home on 16 December. On 30 December, he wrote to Nannerl again, with instructions for what she must do when she journeyed out to be with them. He signed himself:

I am, as always, your Munich.

This is just one of the many fun signoffs which Mozart used. In his next letter, he signed off:

Farewell! A thousand kisses to Bimberl.

Bimberl was Mozart's dog.

Nannerl eventually joined them early in 1775, in time to witness a successful premiere of *La finta giardiniera* on 13 January. Mozart received shouts of

"Viva, Maestro!" and the blessings of the elector
and electoress, while the local bishop sent round his
congratulations the following morning.

When Mozart was nineteen

Salzburg beckoned – or, should we say, there were
no more reasons to be away – and the trio of
Mozarts arrived home on 7 March. Besides, there
was important work to do back home. Archduke
Maximilian was about to visit Colloredo and
Mozart was instructed to provide the music for his
entertainment, which he did. In fact, for the whole
of 1775, Mozart concentrated on his proper job in
Salzburg. His increasing mastery of his art meant
that this was a creative purple patch, particularly
with the five Violin Concertos, composed between
April and December this year. The most well-
known – Nos. 3, 4 and 5 (the *Turkish*) – show his
composing powers developing still further. They
would have been written for him to perform himself
and he would have led the Salzburg court orchestra
from the violin.

When Mozart was twenty

Once again, the Mozarts managed to keep
themselves at home for the whole year. Much like
the previous 12 months, Mozart spent 1776 writing
at his now familiar frantic rate of composition.
Chief among the works that year, though, was

something that was not even composed to be seriously heard. It was Mozart muzak.

Despite his state workload, Mozart often took on other, personal commissions. When a family friend, Siegmund Haffner, approached them with a request for music for his sister's wedding, Mozart happily obliged.

Hard as it might be for us to imagine today, the resulting *Haffner Serenade* was designed to be played to the chatting, eating, drinking guests at Marie Elisabeth Haffner's wedding, on 21 July 1776. Despite this fact, which you might think at least mildly annoying for a composer, the *Haffner Serenade* is, again, one of Mozart's early successes – a great work, full of depth and invention, despite only receiving scant attention from the audience at its first performance.

When Mozart was twenty-one

The year 1777 saw the start of a very long departure from life in Salzburg. Mozart was increasingly frustrated with his home town and, once again, requested leave of absence. Colloredo, one might think fairly, considering the amount of time off he has already given Mozart over the years, refused. He was so annoyed at yet another petition for leave of absence that he sacked both Mozart and Leopold, albeit in a pointedly laconic way:

Father and son are granted permission to find their fortune elsewhere – in accordance with the gospel.

This line, their dismissal, referred to the Mozarts' petition for leave, which had cited the gospel's teaching that you should seek to make use of your talents.

Leopold, ever thoughtful about his long-term security, must have been beside himself. He resigned himself immediately to staying at home and more or less begged for his job back. Mozart, by the same token, decided to leave anyway. As a result, a carriage was hired and, on 23 September, he set out – minus his father but this time with his mother – and headed first for Munich and then Augsburg.

Leopold was born in Augsburg and he still had family there. While he was in the area, Mozart reacquainted himself with his distant cousin, Maria Anna Thekla, whom he affectionately called "Bäsle". She seems to have shared Mozart's sense of humour and they quickly become good friends, possibly even lovers. His letters to her show an awakening in him that suggests he was much like any other 21-year-old in that respect:

I'm kissing your hands, your face, your knees, even your – , in a nutshell, anything you let me kiss!

Eventually, he tore himself away from Bäsle and he and his mother moved on to Mannheim, arriving on 30 October. Almost immediately, he fell in love with another girl.

Aloysia Weber was one of three daughters of a musician and music copyist, Fridolin Weber. (Eventually, Fridolin's brother, Franz, would marry, twice, and his second wife, Genoveva, would give birth to a son, Carl Maria von Weber, the composer. But that was a long way off at this point.) The Webers were a little down on their luck when Mozart met them and it says much for his character – and little for Leopold's – that he took an immediate shine to the family, despite their standing. Leopold, on the other hand, filled his letters of the time with calls for his son to leave them alone – especially Aloysia – and to get on to Paris, to become a celebrity and to make some money.

Leopold's letters have led some people to conclude that he was solely in it for the money – that his son, the child prodigy, was his meal ticket and that he was living the life his own abilities would not otherwise grant him. But this does seem unfair to us. Although he knew the value of his son's talent, Leopold also clearly loved the boy and many of his jottings prove it. For example, he sent this touching letter at this time, while holed up on his own, in Salzburg:

*It makes me sad now and again because I can't hear
you play the piano, or violin . . . Each time I get back
to the house, a slight feeling of melancholy hits me,
because, as I approach, I still half expect to hear the
sound of your violin.*

Despite moments like these, the prevailing tone of
Leopold's letters, though, was one of impatience.
Also, he was aware that his wife was not particularly
well, and he was keen for Mozart to move on to
Paris, on the basis that the sooner they went, the
sooner they would return.

In the end, Mozart ended up staying some
5 months in Mannheim, supposedly trying to get
himself a job. This is almost certainly partly true,
but his attraction to Aloysia was no doubt a big
pull, too.

When Mozart was twenty-two

Mozart eventually dragged himself away from
Mannheim in the spring of 1778, arriving in Paris
at the beginning of April. Little did he know, at this
point, how unhappy a memory his stay in Paris
would become.

As ever, he busied himself with a stream of
networking social functions, always with the eye on
the next commission and, even better, the mythical
"musical post". For a composer to break through in

Paris at the time he would have to have done so by the medium of opera. The opera world in Paris, though, had far too much on its mind to bother with the young man from Salzburg.

Today, classical music lovers are often asked: "Do you prefer Mozart or Beethoven?" Back then, a similar battle being played out in Paris was "Are you for Gluck or Piccinni?" (Piccinni was a fairly well-known Italian composer based in Paris at the time. He is not to be confused with the successful Italian operatic composer, Puccini.) German music was not particularly sought after, although Mozart did receive a commission from the Paris Opéra for some incidental ballet music. Throughout the month of May, he worked on *Les petits riens* and he saw it performed on 11 June. During this period, he was particularly badly treated by the Duchess of Chabot, who seemed to regard him as nothing more than a hired hand, playing for her art class while she and her guests ignored his performances. On 12 June, his *Symphony No. 31 in D* – eventually nicknamed "The Paris Symphony" – freshly written that month, was performed at the home of another local bigwig, Count Sickingen.

Then came the biggest upset of his life so far. His mother died.

She had been unwell since Mannheim, complaining of a bad throat and ear problems and, though keen

for them to get a move on, Leopold refused to countenance her returning home on her own, to recover there. In Paris, things quickly got worse. She began to suffer from chills and a fever, alongside frequent headaches, and she died on 3 July. Mozart decided that he would hide the truth from his father, painting a grim picture, but not giving him all the facts straight away:

They say I should hope, but not much. All day and night, I've switched between hope and fear – although now I've surrendered completely to God's will . . . I'm not saying she will die, or that I've lost all hope – she might recover her health, by God's will.

At the time of writing this, Mozart's mother was already dead. He obviously felt some sort of reversal of responsibility to his ageing father. Somewhat forlorn, Mozart left Paris in the September of that year, stopping off in Munich on the way home, where he found the Webers. They had now moved out of Mannheim and, from Christmas Day, he lodged with them for a while, keen to rekindle his friendship with Aloysia. Alas for him, she appeared to have moved on and was all set to start her new job – as singer at the Munich Opera House. Romance was certainly not in the air.

In the end, his dear old dad rescued him from this particularly unfortunate situation. He wrote for him to return to Salzburg, where Colloredo had agreed

not only to his reinstatement, but also to giving him a new job as court organist on a much bigger salary.

When Mozart was twenty-three

Twenty-three was probably not Mozart's favourite age. He'd arrived back in Salzburg in mid-January with pretty much nothing to keep him away – and nothing on the horizon, either. As of 25 February he was now not only Konzertmeister, but also court organist. His salary was a pretty useful 450 gulden a year, but for this, on top of all his old duties, he now had to play in the chapel and create a huge amount of church music, too. Today, we consider ourselves lucky that Mozart was compelled to write so much music. Being the perfectionist he was, he never composed anything lightly or cheaply, even though he knew he could very easily have done so. As a result, Mozart produced a massive body of works of all varieties: concertos, symphonies, divertimenti and, now, small-scale religious works.

When Mozart's story is told, Colloredo, a little like Leopold, gets a bad press. He is sometimes viewed as being the obnoxious, idly rich, landed gent who treated Mozart with contempt, paid him too little and never appreciated him. We think that this is an unfair summary of the man. Colloredo, if anything, was more musical than his predecessor, Schrattenbach, and did his best to raise the standards of musicianship at Salzburg. He was a violin player himself, who appears to have tried to redirect the Salzburg wealth to benefit as many folk as possible. Admittedly, he was not best liked by his subjects, or even his colleagues. The vote to elect him had had to be taken nearly 50 times until he was finally chosen. He was certainly not loved by the Mozarts, but it does appear that his intentions were good.

Some of the Mozarts' problems with their boss were of their own making. Mozart himself wanted a good, full-time post, outside Salzburg. Wherever he went, he openly and often loudly appealed for new positions, almost certainly with an indiscreet inability to keep his views on Salzburg to himself. As a result, it was no secret to Colloredo that Mozart didn't actually want to be there.

But did Colloredo know what a gem he had in Mozart? Well, probably to some extent, but nobody at the time could have foreseen Mozart's future standing in the music world. Colloredo probably did, however, realize that Mozart was exceptionally able and it could well be that this was why he was so indulgent of him for so long. There was a real value to him in having Mozart tied to Salzburg.

Mozart found his position in society in Salzburg one of the hardest things to deal with and it is hard not to sympathize with him on this. Imagine – when he was away from Salzburg on one of his

tours, Mozart was treated as a phenomenon. First, he was regarded as a child prodigy and then, once he was older, as a fully fledged genius. He mixed with emperors and empresses, with noblemen and with other famous musicians and composers. But back at home in Salzburg, he was merely one of the staff and, as we will see, it was this longing for social status that proved to be the turning point in his story.

When Mozart was twenty-four

The only thing that had brightened up 1779 for Mozart had been a commission from Munich for a new opera. He was now 24. Apart from the opera *Zaide* written a year earlier (for which some of the music no longer exists) the last time Mozart had ventured into opera was around 5 years earlier, when he was still only 19. So, on 5 November 1780, when he left for Munich, he must have felt a burst of excitement. Not only was he was getting away from Salzburg and heading for the bright lights, but he must also have suspected that in his new, so far half-finished opera, *Idomeneo*, he had a hit on his hands.

Before he left, he fulfilled yet another of his duties as court composer and organist, completing the *Solemn Vespers for Soloists, Chorus and Orchestra*. It's a series of six psalms, the penultimate being "*Laudate Dominum*", a beautiful setting of the words "O Praise ye the Lord, Praise Him all ye people" for soprano voice.

His new opera, *Idomeneo*, had come as a commission from the elector of Bavaria, who was now resident in Munich. Mozart had probably completed the recitatives before leaving home. He would then have moved to Munich to complete the arias, only after having met and practised with the singers. Mozart was always keen to hear how a person could sing before he would write an aria for them.

All went well with *Idomeneo* and Mozart took the cast through the first rehearsals in December.

When Mozart was twenty-five

The first dress rehearsal of *Idomeneo* coincided with Mozart's 25th birthday. Sometime between then and the premiere, his father Leopold arrived in Munich with Nannerl. The first night – the only night, to be fair – went very well. Mozart had achieved the success that he had hoped for, although the opera would not be performed again for another 5 years.

Unsurprisingly, the Mozarts took the opportunity to stay in Munich until sometime in March. They travelled back home at a leisurely pace, stopping off to see relatives in Augsburg. Colloredo had in the

meantime travelled to Vienna and ordered Mozart
to join him there. Even though he was fast realizing
that it was Colloredo he disliked more than the
parochial Salzburg, Mozart did not need to be asked
twice and he bade his family farewell. This decision
to move to Vienna was a seismic moment in
Mozart's life. He would never call Salzburg home
again.

On the morning of 16 March 1781, Mozart duly
arrived in Vienna. His first official duty was to play
at a concert for Colloredo that afternoon. At
lunchtime, Mozart was dismayed to find himself
seated with the servants. He regarded this as a great
insult. In the court pecking order, he was below

How did Mozart compose?

*Sammy Cahn, the man who wrote the words for many of
Frank Sinatra's biggest hits, once said that he was often asked:
"Which comes first – the music or the words?" He always
replied: "The phone call." He would adapt and react to
almost any situation, as long as the commission was right.*

*Mozart was not dissimilar, with the exception of one major
aspect. Yes, he would always write specifically for a
commission. But he did have certain methods of composing
that he held to almost all his life. Chief among these was his
practice of "composing in his head".*

*Much of Mozart's life was spent on the road. These days, as
any commuter will tell you, it is hard enough to write
anything legible on a modern train or coach. In Mozart's day,*

the valets, who were placed at the head of his table. He wrote acidly:

I guess I at least sat above the cooks!

To add insult to injury, Colloredo would not allow him to perform at the big concert of the week at the Countess Thun's residence, which was attended by the emperor. It clashed with Mozart's duties to play for Colloredo, in honour of the archbishop's father. He requested time to see Colloredo, but was instead granted a meeting with his deputy, Arco. In this infamous meeting, by all accounts a slanging match, it appeared that Mozart suddenly realized that he had gone too far with his complaints.

the coach system made it all but impossible. It might have been this that led Mozart to do much of his composing in his head. He would spend, for example, an achingly tough journey to Prague, bouncing up and down on the rough roads and tracks, thinking out his music in his mind.

When he arrived at his destination, he would take his pen and paper and write out a more or less finished work that had been stored inside his brain and just needed transcribing. Remember, Mozart was a child prodigy so, despite his often juvenile reputation, he had not only a brilliant musical mind but also, simply, a brilliant mind, period. His memory was formidable and this allowed him to use his years of travelling time to their fullest.

His relationship with his boss had completely broken down and, sensing that he was about to be sacked, he jumped before he could be pushed, resigning on the spot. Arco was incensed – probably because he had not had the satisfaction of sacking Mozart – and he literally booted him up the backside and out the door. It was 8 June 1781. Mozart was on his own.

05

The Adult Composer

This is surely piano country.

Thus wrote Mozart to his father in 1781, noting
that, in the salons of Vienna, the piano was king.
Indeed, it is no accident that in all 25 years of
his life so far, he had composed a respectable ten
piano concertos but that, in the next ten, up to his
death in 1791, he would compose a further 17.
Bearing in mind that Mozart didn't compose
on a whim, it's clear that he realized not only the
dominance of the piano in Vienna at the time, but
how this dominance could be made to work in his
favour.

The ever-travelling Weber family – last seen in Munich, and now minus the departed Fridolin – had, by this time, moved to Vienna. Mozart was more than happy to lodge with them in St Peter's Square. He had no hopes of rekindling his affair with Aloysia, who was now married, but his eyes did wander onto her younger sister, Constanze. Before long, he was in love again.

Constanze was, in many ways, the perfect partner for Mozart. She was probably more than a match for his sometimes flighty, left-field humour; she was down to earth; she could run a house well. Mozart found her attractive, although he played down this point to his father:

She's only pretty in that she has two small black eyes and a good figure.

Leopold was not fooled, though. He knew he would be hearing more of this Constanze woman.

With the value of hindsight, this was probably one of the happiest periods in Mozart's life. He was free of Colloredo; he was living in Vienna; he was in love and there was a huge potential for new work. He had pupils; he had a publisher (the famous Artaria and Company); he was giving concerts; *and* he was busy. Just to add the icing to the cake, at the end of July, a libretto for an opera was placed in his hand. It was written by one of the actors from the

Vienna Burgtheater called Johann Stephanie and was an adaptation of a play from the previous year, *Belmonte and Constanze*. This would become the opera *The Abduction from the Harem*. The heroine was called Constanze and the irony of this would not have been lost on Mozart.

His profile was already rising even though he had only been in Vienna for a few months. By December, he was "famous" enough to be invited to a duel.

Another pianist had arrived in town, as Mozart wrote to Leopold:

Yesterday, on the 24th, I played piano at court. Another piano player, an Italian called Clementi, is in Vienna. He was there too. I got 50 ducats for my troubles, and, right now, I need them.

Mozart is being a little economical with the truth. The encounter with Clementi wasn't quite so innocuous. Clementi was himself a supremely regarded pianist, and, on this occasion, had been invited to court as part of the general merrymaking surrounding the presence of the Grand Duke and Duchess of Russia. Mozart and Clementi were asked to become musical gladiators for the court's entertainment, and engaged in a contest of piano virtuosity, reading of music at first sight and general musical improvisation. Mozart came off best and this undoubtedly did his reputation the power of good, as his opponent was a very well-respected composer and performer at the time.

When Mozart was twenty-six

Mozart's mind continued to be occupied with two things: composing his new opera and romancing Miss Weber. He also found himself having to fend off his increasingly curmudgeonly dad in his letters. It would be easy to read Leopold's letters and gain the impression that his son was a disappointing dropout rather than an increasingly famous composer. Leopold didn't let up the pressure on Mozart in these years and it was to Mozart's credit that he never completely lost his temper with his father.

Eventually, after a few months of pussyfooting around the general subject of Constanze, Mozart came right out with the news that he was going to get married, in a letter to Leopold:

I've decided to, first, make sure I've got some money coming in – it's not too hard to survive here with the odd Godsend – and then, to get married . . . But who's the girl I love? Well, don't blow your top. "Surely not one of the Webers?" Yes, actually, one of the Webers. Not Josepha, not Sophie . . . Constanze!

It must have hit Leopold for six. Having already managed to keep Mozart from getting too attached

to one member of the Weber family, he ended up marrying another.

By 16 July 1782, the new opera, *The Abduction from the Harem*, was ready and it was premiered at the Burgtheater, in the presence of the emperor, netting Mozart a much-needed 100 ducats. Lovers of the film *Amadeus*, which is discussed in Chapter 10, might remember the much-quoted moment in the movie where the emperor approached Mozart after this very premiere and semi-praised him:

Too beautiful for our ears, Herr Mozart, my dear Mozart, and far too many notes!

To which Mozart quickly replied:

Just as many as are necessary, your Majesty!

The exchange did happen, apparently. The remainder of July and August saw Mozart taken up with his imminent nuptials and new commissions. A friend of the Mozart family, Siegmund Haffner, was being given a gong by the goodly people of Vienna. When Leopold asked Mozart to write him a symphony, Mozart was only too happy to fulfil the commission, partly for Haffner, but probably more to keep his father happy.

Mozart's wedding day was on 4 August 1782. He and Constanze were married at the impressive

St Stephen's Cathedral, a very grand building, which was effectively their local church.

Just a few weeks into his marriage, although blissfully happy with Constanze, he was already having trouble with the mother-in-law. When explaining his domestic situation in a letter to his father, he wrote:

You say that I never mentioned on which floor I'm living? . . . I live on the second floor. I don't know how you got the impression we lived with my mother-in-law. I didn't marry Constanze in order to live a life of arguments and squabbles. There's only one way to do that – move away from the family. We've been to see her twice since the wedding and, the second time, the rebukes and arguments began – Constanze started crying. I told her it was time to leave.

There you are. Mozart, the genius, the prodigy, probably the world's greatest composer . . . and he had mother-in-law trouble!

For the rest of the year, Mozart concentrated on more musical matters. He himself conducted another performance of *The Abduction from the Harem* at the Burgtheater in October, again in honour of the Russian grand duke. In November, there was a concert at which he played, along with his pupil, Josepha Auernhammer, at Vienna's

Kärtnerthortheater. Sadly, though, Mozart put off
a visit to Salzburg to celebrate his father's nameday.
In a letter dated 22 January 1782, Mozart also
asked his father to send on from Salzburg a
harlequin suit that he wanted for the carnival
celebrations. He also mentioned a big party they
threw in their new lodgings:

*Last week, we threw our own party . . . It started at six
in the evening and ended at seven. What, an hour? No,
seven the next morning! . . . Baron Wezlar and his wife
were there, the Waldstattens, von Edelbach . . . I can't
possibly remember them all!*

For so long Leopold had lived his life vicariously
through his son, but with his wife now long gone,
he must have felt that his own life had changed
completely.

When Mozart was twenty-seven

No longer newly weds, and now living in a new flat,
Mozart continued to devote himself to his new life
as, more or less, one of the world's first freelance
composers. Always keen to mix business with
pleasure, he performed a *Masquerade*, with the help
of friends, in the interval of a masked ball at the
Vienna's famous Redoutensaal ballroom. This
proved to be a precursor to a full concert of his
music on 11 March. Even taking into account the

likelihood that Mozart would wish to talk it up
to his father, it does appear to have been a huge
success:

*I guess I don't need to tell you about how well the
concert went, as you've probably heard already. The
theatre couldn't have been more packed and all
the boxes were taken. Best of all, though – his
Majesty the Emperor loved it and applauded me
wildly!*

Mozart was beginning to be talked about in Vienna.
All he had to do now was sustain this level of
interest. This would not have been easy for Mozart,
as he was effectively his own concert promoter as
well as the star of the show. As such, he had a
choice to make. He could sit and wait for
commissions to come his way or, alternatively, he
could push himself forward into the limelight and
force the issue. His choice of the latter pathway
appeared to be paying early dividends.

At home, at the time of his concert in front of the
emperor, Constanze would have been 6 months
pregnant, and, on 17 June 1783, she gave birth to
a baby boy, whom they named Raimund Leopold:

*Mon très cher Père,
Congratulations, you're a grandad. Early yesterday . . .
at half past six in the morning, my darling wife gave
birth to a fine, big, strapping, plump boy!*

It seems odd to us now, but the Mozarts took a trip to Salzburg to see Leopold, leaving Raimund Leopold behind in Vienna while he was still a young baby. While they were away, their son died and the Mozarts headed back to Vienna. On the way, their coach called in at Linz, where Mozart quickly realized that if he could write a symphony there and then, there would be an opportunity to have it performed in a concert in the Linz theatre. And so that is exactly what he did. Within days, it was completed and was then played at a concert on 4 November. Incidentally, many years later, Linz changed the name of its main town square to reflect Mozart's connection with the city. The name was changed again, in the first half of the 20th century to reflect an altogether different kind of world-famous figure – Adolf Hitler. It was changed back again after the end of the Second World War.

Eventually, the couple returned to Vienna, sad and exhausted. In fact, Mozart himself was quite ill, possibly with a viral infection. The year that had begun so well with carnivals and balls ended with bereavement and illness.

When Mozart was twenty-eight

Mozart and Constanze, childless again, moved from their flat in Judenplatz to a new place in the Trattenerhof area of Vienna. As both a sign of his growing confidence and with an eye to posterity,

Mozart set himself a new task. From 9 February onwards, he would begin to compile the name and the date of every work he had ever written into a thematic catalogue. Or as he put it, his:

list of all my works from February 1784 to the month 1___ . Wolfgang Amadé Mozart, by my own hand.

In this title to his catalogue, Mozart left the end date blank, save for the first digit, the "1", and many a scholar has reflected on the fact that, at this point, no one would have foreseen that the next number entered would also be a 7, meaning that this great talent would be snuffed out before the end of the 18th century. In this catalogue, Mozart jotted down a brief theme of each work alongside the date and title and, in some cases, the performers.

During the Lenten season of 1784, Mozart performed a series of 17 concerts by means of subscription. Subscription was a popular way of self-promoting a concert, which meant that the composer was not out of pocket. Interested parties were persuaded to part with a set amount of money each – often in return for a score of the work performed, often out of pure philanthropy – and the composer or performer would use this money to cover his costs.

In August of this year, Mozart's sister, Nannerl, was married, to Johann Baptist von Berchtold zu

Sonnenburg, a local magistrate. Much as it might have been nice for her to "pull a few strings" and use some of her brother's music for the wedding, Mozart was unable to attend, because of commitments in Vienna. As Mozart said in his letter to her:

Sorry we can't be there at the wedding. But we should be able to visit you in St Gilgen in the spring. Our only sadness is that dear father is now left so totally alone!

The same month, while attending an opera by the composer, Paisiello, in Vienna, Mozart was struck down with an attack of colic during the performance. His doctor, Sigmund Barisani, was called and quickly diagnosed rheumatic fever. Mozart suffered similar attacks for 4 days on the trot and was ill with a fever until September, when he started to make a good recovery.

He was better just in time, too – because rheumatic fever would not have been good for a baby. On 21 September, Constanze gave birth to their second child, Carl. Unlike his brother Raimund, Carl would live to the ripe old age of 74. Very early in his life, his parents moved house, again. This time it was to the much more salubrious Domgasse. And salubriousness brought with it expense, with the flat costing the Mozarts a staggering 450 gulden a year.

The close of 1784 saw Mozart being invited to join a masonic lodge. His friend and loyal patron, Otto von Gemmingen, was the master of a lodge called "Beneficence" and he put forward Mozart's name as a suitable candidate for membership. It would not be long before Mozart had introduced both his father and his friend, the composer Haydn, into freemasonry. Indeed, certain parts of his musical output would begin to reflect his membership of the lodge, culminating in the completely masonic opera, *The Magic Flute*, in the year before he died. For now, though, it was quartets that were on Mozart's mind and, in the New Year, he proudly played his latest ones to Haydn at his house in the Domgasse. Today, many musicians regard Haydn as the absolute master when it came to composing for quartets.

When Mozart was twenty-nine

The New Year brought a new visitor to the Mozart household in Vienna. Leopold upped sticks from Salzburg to visit his son in his plush pad on the Domgasse. He was in time to witness Mozart giving the first of a series of "Friday Concerts", where he played his stunning *Piano Concerto No. 20*.

The concert clashed with the initiation of Haydn into another masonic lodge, "True Concord", so it was the following evening when both Leopold's visit and Haydn's initiation were celebrated at the Domgasse apartment with the playing of three more quartets. Things were going well for Mozart. He was giving concerts left right and centre – five in February, six in March – and his writing had taken on a fresh insight.

Mozart's piano concertos, more than any other type of work he wrote, highlight his development as a composer. They are often said to form the backbone of his output: he wrote his first when he was just 17 and continued composing new ones right up to the year he died. Some musicologists also believe that you can see his mastery of the orchestra develop more easily in his piano concertos than you can by listening to his symphonies. Generally, his piano concertos were written for him to perform himself and the early ones, while displaying flashes of genius, reveal someone very keen to show off his keyboard skills. By the time we reach the later concertos, Mozart's musical thinking is on a whole new level.

Eventually, in early April, Leopold himself was initiated into his son's masonic lodge, and, as if by way of thanks, Mozart wrote the cantata *Die Maurerfreude*. It was set to a libretto by Franz Petran that praised Emperor Joseph II for his kind treatment of the masons. The key of its setting,

E Flat, would have signified "wisdom" to Mozart and his fellow masons.

In fact, 1785 was really *the* year in which all things masonic kicked off for Mozart. When his father returned to Salzburg at the end of April, Mozart went on to perform more lodge music later that year, in both November and December. As well as relying on the significance of musical keys, Mozart also highlighted certain instruments with masonic links, such as the basset-horn.

Mozart began an important commission in October 1785, for an opera with a libretto by Lorenzo da Ponte, called *The Marriage of Figaro*. Mozart and da Ponte chose to base their work on a play that had already scandalized half of Europe. Indeed, it was actually banned in Germany. Da Ponte was forced to hold meetings with the emperor personally to assure him that he had taken out any bits that might offend too much. Today, it is very easy for us to say what composers would and would not write if they were around in the 21st century, but it is worth noting that if he were alive today, parts of Mozart's output would have been seen as cutting-edge stuff that pushed back the boundaries.

It certainly looked as if life was going swimmingly for Mozart back in 1785. With his prolific rate of composition and concert performance coupled with the influential company that he now kept he would be able, as Leopold had revealed to his sister in a letter earlier in the year:

to bank 2000 gulden. The money is definitely there.

The year drew to a close with yet more good news: Mozart's portrait was to be included in two new calendars being published in Vienna. And we think that "branding" is a 20th-century phenomenon. So, while he was still in his twenties, Mozart had the potential to be both rich and famous. Surely then, things could not possibly all go wrong?

And yet, before this year had the chance to end, Mozart was already writing a letter to his friend and fellow mason, Franz Hoffmeister:

I beg you . . . can you help me out with just a little money? At the moment, I'm in dire need.

It was to be the first of many such letters.

When Mozart was thirty

Despite already working on *The Marriage of Figaro*, Mozart had taken on a new opera commission in the January of 1786. His decision was no doubt influenced by the request coming from the emperor himself, in honour of the emperor's sister.

When the emperor said "Compose!" . . . Mozart
composed.

The same wordsmith who was behind *The
Abduction from the Harem* provided Mozart with
the libretto. Emperor Joseph II himself provided
him with the welcome sum of 50 ducats. In turn,
Mozart provided everyone with an opera called
The Impresario. It premiered in the Orangery
of Schönbrunn Castle on 7 February, and later
transferred to the Kärtnerthortheater for a
further three performances. Add to this a repeat
performance of his opera *Idomeneo* at the palace of
Prince Auersperg and concertgoers had the perfect
warm-up season for the main event in the Mozart
calendar of 1786. This came on 1 May, the date of
the premiere of *The Marriage of Figaro* at Vienna's
Burgtheater:

The Marriage of Figaro *will be performed for the first
time . . . It's going to be important, if it succeeds,
because it's well known that there are incredibly strong
factions against it. Salieri and his cohorts will try to
move heaven and earth.*

So wrote Leopold to Nannerl on 18 April
of this year. He need not have worried. *The
Marriage of Figaro* was a huge success and the
future of the Mozart name looked set to be
golden.

However, this was not quite the case where his father was concerned. Leopold had begun to realize that Mozart would soon bankrupt himself if he continued with his lavish lifestyle. Earlier in the year, he had written to Nannerl:

As you can imagine, your brother's flat is decorated exquisitely, with all mod cons – as befits somewhere costing 480 gulden.

It had not gone unnoticed by Leopold that his son's rent constituted a rise of 300% on one of Mozart's previous homes. As a result, relations between Leopold and Mozart were at a bit of a low ebb. Bearing this in mind, it was unsurprising that, when Mozart was considering a trip to England around this time, Leopold refused point blank to agree to a request from his son and daughter-in-law to look after baby Carl while they were away. Some scholars have presented this decision as one of the great "what ifs?" of Mozart's final years. What if Leopold had agreed to care for Carl? Would Mozart have made money on the tour of England, as Haydn did so famously, just under 5 years later? In our view, the answer is "probably not". Mozart was, by then, spending permanently beyond his means.

In October, Constanze gave birth to a third child, Johann, but, sadly, he survived for only a month. Mozart took his mind off yet another tragic loss by

setting up arrangements to visit Prague, for the planned premiere there of *The Marriage of Figaro*. As Leopold explained to Nannerl:

Your brother and his wife will be in Prague by now . . . So successful was The Marriage of Figaro *that the [Prague] orchestra and a group of distinguished connoisseurs . . . sent him a letter, inviting him.*

In early January 1787 Mozart and Constanze travelled to Prague, where the opera repeated its Viennese success. If anything, the reception surpassed anything he had previously been accorded. He took with him a new symphony, which was completed just a month earlier, especially for his visit to the city. His *Symphony No. 39* became known as *The Prague Symphony*. Music lovers in the city appeared to hold a soft spot for Mozart and his work. He soon agreed with the Prague impresario, Pasquale Bondini, that he would start work almost straight away on a new opera, again with da Ponte as the librettist, based on the story of Don Juan.

When Mozart was thirty-one

On 7 April 1787 a 17-year-old composer arrived fresh in Vienna. By all accounts, he was already familiar with Mozart's music and was minded to meet up with him. It's said he played music with him and even, possibly, had some lessons from him. The young composer's name was

Ludwig van Beethoven. He was yet to settle in
Vienna full time, but was eager to make his mark.

For Mozart, though, this was a tricky time because
his financial problems were beginning to catch up
with him. He was forced to move his family out of
their beautiful, but cripplingly expensive Domgasse
apartment to a much cheaper place in the
Landstrasse, which was further away from the city
centre. Mozart became unwell again. It is not
exactly clear what was wrong with him, but it was
enough for him to call out Barisani again, this time
to his Landstrasse flat. Despite his own personal
health and money problems, Mozart still found it in
himself to loan around 300 gulden to a close friend
in need. The money was never paid back.

Tragically for Mozart, though, he was about to
come into money in a manner in which he would
rather not. On 28 May 1787 Leopold Mozart died.
When all his affairs were taken care of, Mozart
received 1000 gulden from his father's estate. It was
a much-needed financial boost.

In October, Mozart and Constanze set out on their
journey to Prague, to oversee rehearsals for the new
opera, *Don Giovanni.* By his own account, it was a
gruelling period for Mozart:

*I've been writing this letter for eleven days now . . .
whenever I can, I grab a moment to pen a few more*

lines, but I don't often get very long. I'm too much at the beck and call of others, and too little at my own . . . not a state of affairs I would choose of my own accord. The opera will be premiered next Monday, the 29th. The following day, I'll tell you how it went.

It was duly premiered on 29th October, with Mozart himself conducting four performances. It was a staggering success. By the time he returned to Vienna, he had been given a new job: Kammermusicus to the Emperor's court. The job did not require much from one so great as Mozart but it did guarantee him 800 gulden as a regular income. Constanze gave birth to a baby girl, Theresia, in December, so Mozart had one more mouth to feed. By this time, he had already written several begging letters to his friend and fellow mason, Michael Puchberg, and he was very much in debt. To be fair, Mozart's problems with money were more to do with cash flow than lack of earnings but, nevertheless, by this time, he was in quite some financial disarray.

When Mozart was thirty-two

There is a rather melancholic Frank Sinatra song that was a big hit for the blue-eyed crooner, in which every verse includes the line "It was a very good year". Well, sad to say, for Mozart, 1788 was *not* a very good year.

In May, *Don Giovanni* received its premiere in Vienna, after its huge success in Prague. Amazingly, for the opera that many consider not only to be Mozart's best, but also a contender for the title of history's best, *Don Giovanni* failed. In an attempt to make money, Mozart decided to publish three quintets, by subscription, but not enough subscribers were found and the initiative left him further in the red. To bring his dire financial straits to a head, a lucrative series of concerts he had been giving in Vienna also came to an end.

No doubt all these financial woes paled into insignificance against the news of 29 June. Mozart's daughter, Theresia, died aged only 6 months. Despite infant mortality being commonplace at the time, each death was no less distressing for the parents.

As the year wore on, the bulk of Mozart's surviving correspondence consists of letters to people such as his friend Puchberg, along the lines of this one:

If you could possibly be kind enough to lend me around one or two thousand gulden, over one or two years, at a suitable rate of interest, you really would be doing me a favour.

Or this one:

I haven't the heart to be in your company because I'd be obliged to admit that I can't possibly pay you back

*what you're owed, and I beg you to be patient with me.
I'm so sorry.*

> Mozart must have been glad to see the back of
> 1788.

When Mozart was thirty-three

> There was no end to Mozart's financial
> predicament. In April 1789 he wrote this letter to
> a friend who was a judge:

*I'm taking the liberty of writing, with no airs and
graces, to ask a favour. Can you lend me 100 gulden
until 20th May – that's when I get paid, and I'll be
able to give you it back.*

> It is heartbreaking to think that Mozart, the great
> composer, was reduced to writing letters that were
> so desperate.

> Between April and June this year, Mozart
> accompanied Prince Lichnowsky on his travels to
> Germany. They stopped at various places en route,
> including Dresden, Leipzig, Potsdam and Berlin.
> In Dresden, Mozart had his portrait painted, but
> found the women not all he might have hoped for:

*It was a big group, consisting entirely of ugly women,
but they make up for their lack of beauty here by
virtue.*

In Leipzig, he played the organ of St Thomas's Church, where Johann Sebastian Bach previously worked. In Berlin, Friedrich Wilhelm II offered him the post of chief Kapellmeister, on a salary that might almost certainly have meant an end to his financial problems. Mozart's response was to turn it down. It is claimed that he said to a friend:

I do like Vienna . . . the Emperor is good to me and I'm not particularly bothered about money.

Back in Vienna, he was reunited with Constanze, who had been prevented from accompanying him to Germany because she was pregnant once again. Another daughter, Anna Maria, was born in November but, again, she did not survive.

It was reportedly around this time, on his return to Vienna, that Emperor Joseph II suggested that Mozart get together with da Ponte to work on another opera. This time, he suggested, they should write on the subject of two men who test the faithfulness of their wives. Da Ponte created a completely original libretto that was not based on any other play or book. Mozart set to work writing the music.

Whether the subject matter of what was to become *Così fan tutte* was preying on his mind is hard to tell, but it was around this time that Mozart had

a rare occasion to reprimand his wife, for what he perceived to be her "too compliant" behaviour:

I'm glad you're happy – obviously – but I just wish you wouldn't sometimes make yourself so cheap!

It was a rare moment of discontent in an otherwise loving and devoted series of letters.

December saw the premiere of the Mozart's *Clarinet Quintet*, which was performed a few days before Christmas at the Viennese Society of Musicians. And on New Year's Eve, Mozart found a small way of rewarding Puchberg by inviting him to the first, private rehearsal of his new opera, *Così fan tutte*, alongside his great friend Haydn.

The main rehearsals began at the Burgtheater on 21 January. Again, Haydn and Puchberg were invited. The opera went well and the premiere was a success. Despite this, *Così fan tutte* received relatively few performances during Mozart's lifetime beyond its original first run.

When Mozart was thirty-four

On 20 February 1790 Mozart's words in Berlin must have been ringing in his ears. Back then he had told a friend: "The Emperor is good to me and I'm not bothered about money." Tragically, on 20 February Emperor Joseph II, the man who had personally suggested the subject matter for Mozart's last opera, died. He was replaced by his brother, Leopold. Mozart applied for a better job at court – second Kapellmeister. Amidst the upheaval, he was hopeful that he might be successful. By then, his letters to Puchberg had taken on an added significance:

Stick with me, as much as you can. You can imagine how my present circumstances would ruin my chances of my application to the court, if anyone found out.

So Mozart was now not only reduced to borrowing money, but also to begging his lender not to let anyone know that he was doing it. So far as it is possible to tell, Puchberg, already a true friend to Mozart as a moneylender, continued to be a good friend as a confidant, too. Sadly for Mozart, news eventually came through to him that he had not got the job.

In June Mozart himself was given the task of conducting his most recent opera, *Così fan tutte*, in a rerun at the Burgtheater. He was given some more work by another of his sometime patrons, Baron von Swieten, who was putting on his own summer concert series. Mozart was hired to adapt some oratorios by Handel for the performance.

In September he, like many others, travelled to Frankfurt, for the coronation of Leopold II. He was

accompanied by his brother-in-law, Franz Hofer,
a one-time violinist at St Stephen's and now a court
fiddler. While he was away travelling, Constanze
was forced to move with Carl into a yet smaller, less
expensive flat.

Once in Frankfurt, in October, Mozart gave a
concert, but it was poorly attended and did little
to fill the coffers. He continued his mini-tour
on to Mannheim, where he witnessed a German
performance of *The Marriage of Figaro*. From there,
it was on to Munich in early November, where he
played in front of the king of Naples. Despite what
must have been increasing concerns about money,
he managed some moments of fun and frivolity in a
letter to his wife:

*Catch — an amazing number of kisses are flying
about! . . . I can see a whole host of them, too. I've
just snatched three . . . mmm, delicious!*

There was no inkling of what was to come in 1791.

06

The Final Year

When Mozart was thirty-five

Mozart approached the year 1791 as he had done
any other. He would have been nervous with regard
to his finances; frustrated when it came to his job;
but, at the same time, he tended to be optimistic
about life in general. And the dawning of 1791 gave
him no cause to think there was any reason to
change. He was more or less at a creative peak, he
was in good health and he was very happily
married. True, he did not have the ideal job, but in
his heart, he always believed that this was just
around the corner.

In Vienna, each year usually ended with court
balls and so Mozart, as one of the court
composers, was required to supply dance music.
He treated the task with all the care and attention
that he would have lavished on his greatest works
and many of his minuets and dances continued
to be popular in the great dance halls of Vienna –
primarily the Redoutensaal – even after his
death.

April

Just as had been the case in the previous few years,
many of Mozart's letters concerned the need for
money. He had played his last public concert on
4 March and just over a month later was clearly
beginning to feel the pinch again. On 13 April,
he fired off a letter to the seemingly ever-faithful
Puchberg, his fellow mason, asking for just a
small loan:

*I'll get my quarterly pay on the 20th – is there any
chance you'll lend me something like 20 gulden? If you
can, I'd be much obliged, best friend, and, as soon as
I'm paid, I'll give it back to you.*

There's a note scribbled at the bottom of the letter,
in Puchberg's handwriting, which reads:

Sent 30 gulden, 13th April

By sending more money than Mozart had requested and by dispatching it the very same day, Puchberg was proving to be a very true friend indeed.

April was to bring more hope to Mozart in the form of Leopold Hofmann. He was a 61-year-old composer who had, for some time, held the top job of Kapellmeister at St Stephen's Cathedral in Vienna. In April 1791 Mozart found out that Hofmann was seriously ill. Mozart wrote to the city magistrates, who controlled the jobs at St Stephen's, suggesting that, given Hofmann's somewhat tenuous grasp on good health, they consider taking on Mozart as an unpaid assistant, on the understanding that Mozart take over as soon as the old man was gone.

The job paid some 2000 gulden a year and, with all due respect to Mr Hofmann, his early departure would have made a huge difference to the Mozart family finances. Ironically, Hofmann was set to become yet another name added to the long list that is "people who outlived Mozart". Despite his illness, he was still around a good 2 years after Mozart had gone.

Nevertheless, the city magistrates agreed to the unpaid appointment on 28 April. Nowadays, Mozart is not specifically remembered for his church music, but this – and, perhaps, the course of religious music in general – might have been different had he survived long enough to become the boss of such an important a cathedral as St Stephen's.

May

By May 1791 Constanze would have been around 6 months pregnant with their son, Franz. She was keen to take the restful spa waters of Baden, just a few miles outside Vienna. Mozart wrote to his friend in Baden, the schoolteacher Anton Stoll, who was also director of music at the Baden parish church, to arrange for her accommodation:

Please arrange for a small apartment for my wife. She only needs a couple of rooms – or a room and a small chamber. The main thing is, though, it needs to be on the ground floor. I'd really like it to be the one on the ground floor, at the butcher's . . . She'll be there on Saturday – Monday at the latest. It's important that it is near the baths, but more important that it is on the ground floor. The one at the town clerk's, on the ground floor, would be fine too, but the one at the butcher's would be better.

As if aware of the curiously mundane nature of his writing, Mozart adds:

PS, this is the silliest letter I've ever written in my life – but it's just right for you.

June

Constanze left on 4 June, with little Carl, and Mozart missed her madly. Despite the fact that he

was in perfectly good health physically, it has been suggested that his mental state was somewhat dark and that he may have been beginning to suffer some sort of breakdown. Certainly, he found the separation from Constanze harder to bear than normal. His letters to her in Baden were still filled with the usual sweet nothings:

Farewell, then, my one and only. Take these as they fly through the air: 2999 and a half kisses are flying, eager to be snapped up. Now, let me tell you something in your ear [Mozart leaves a space] and now you me [he leaves another space]. Now, let's open and close our mouths [another space] ever more [space] and more [space] at last we say: it's because of Plumpi-Strumpi . . . Farewell, a thousand tender kisses from, always your Mozart.

The letters also suggest that Mozart was, at this time, less able to be alone than ever before. Take, for example, this note from July that year, which goes beyond the normal lovers' talk:

You won't be able to imagine how long it's felt without you. It's impossible to explain, it's a certain emptiness – painful – a certain longing which can't be satisfied and, consequently, doesn't stop. It just keeps on and on, getting bigger each day.

In the end, despite the potential precariousness of the family finances, Mozart felt compelled to join

121

his wife and son in June 1791. He was held up by his promise to take part in a Viennese concert, which was then ultimately postponed. Mozart wrote again on 6 June, this time revealing that he had been composing:

Out of sheer boredom, I wrote an aria for my opera, today.

The opera in question was to become *The Magic Flute*.

Once out in Baden with his family, Mozart settled a little. He obliged his friend Stoll – who had arranged Constanze's accommodation – with a little something for his parish church choir. The manuscript is dated 17 June 1791 and it was first performed on the feast of Corpus Christi. It is a deceptively simple piece, which has since become one of Mozart's best-loved works.

When heard alongside his *Requiem*, which was soon to follow, it is easy to see why musical historians have wondered over the years since, what Mozart's contribution to church music would have been had he had lived longer. Many music lovers feel certain that, had he lived, Mozart's church music would have changed the face of the genre completely. The simple yet profoundly beautiful nature of the *Ave verum corpus*, in particular, has led some to suggest that he was on the verge of revealing a whole new style of church music to the world.

July

The last 12 months of Mozart's life are often cast as a time of darkness for the composer. It is too simple to say that he was effectively "dying" all year long. Money troubles were nothing new for Mozart, but if anything, there appeared to be more light than shade at the end of the financial tunnel for him. He was very much in love with his wife, as we have seen. There was no sign either, as yet, of any major illness. Against this backdrop, then, the appearance in July of a messenger, asking for a commission for his boss, was probably not the sinister, spooky affair that some versions of the Mozart legend now insist to be the case.

Mozart had been working on his latest opera, *The Magic Flute*, for much of the year. In it, he would pay tribute to many of the principles and practices of the masons, incorporating many masonic symbols into the plot. By July, however, it is most likely he had completed it and maybe even had some parts of his next opera, *La clemenza di Tito* (*The Clemency of Titus*), sketched out or finished too.

The so-called "mysterious" messenger visited Mozart back at home in Vienna and asked him how long it would take him to write a requiem for his master.

Who was that masked man?

The mysterious messenger and his anonymous boss have given dramatists, conspiracy theorists and even Hollywood producers more than enough ammunition over the years to weave a dark tapestry of shadowy, sinister tales surrounding the "masked man". Right up there on the grassy knoll is "the devil". Yes, some say the mystery man was the devil's emissary who was making Mozart write his own requiem before his death. The less said about that, the better. Let's move on.

Something to do with Salieri? Now this one is far too tempting for people to leave alone. Salieri and Mozart were great rivals as composers and it is true to say that they had

A musical Taj Mahal

Franz von Walsegg was a count. A rich, musical man, he owned some lovely land and estates around the River Enns in Austria. He employed a number of servants and staff at his residences. He was particularly proud of his musicians, with whom he whiled away many an affluent afternoon, playing arrangements of various pieces of music that had, at some point, taken his fancy. He, himself, played the cello.

Not content with simply playing music, Walsegg was keen to be seen to compose music too. The mere fact that he actually couldn't compose was not going to stop him. He commissioned many people, over the years, to write him music, which he then copied out, in his own handwriting. Almost always, the true composer's name was missing from his version of the score. When folk asked him who composed the work, he would apparently smile, blush, and let those around

a strong dislike for each other. So, some conspiracy theorists claim that Salieri commissioned the Requiem, which he might then be able to pass off as his own, once he had murdered Mozart. Although the story is undoubtedly an attractive one, we would like to consign that one to the bottom of the basket, too.

The true identity of the commissioner of the Requiem is now actually known to be Count Franz von Walsegg. In its own way, the true story of how it came to be written is quite intriguing enough in itself, without all of the layers of conspiracy being placed on top.

him infer that it was his own work, although he appears to have fooled very few.

When Walsegg's beloved wife died at the age of just 20, he was grief-stricken. He decided to do two things to commemorate her life. He commissioned the respected sculptor, Johann Fischer, to make an epitaph to his wife. Once complete, it was positioned near to his castle in Stuppach, Austia. He also decided to commission a requiem for her, which would be played every year on the anniversary of her death. For this, only the best composer would be good enough. And so he decided to approach Mozart.

It is probably true to say that he intended to pass the work off as his own, although the Requiem was such a strong piece of music, that it is even more doubtful than usual that anyone would have believed him. And besides, he was, sadly, never to get his requiem finished by Mozart anyway.

Mozart told him that he was due to go to Prague for the coronation of the new emperor, Leopold, as King of Bohemia, and was to contribute an opera to the general festivities. (The plot of *La clemenza di Tito*, which centred on the leniency and moderation of its hero, was obviously considered a suitable match for the enlightened character of the new emperor.) Therefore, he could only start work on a requiem when he returned. This was agreed.

Mozart and the messenger also agreed that the work, when complete, was to be owned by its commissioner. They settled on a fee, with which the messenger returned some days later, adding that his boss had considered the payment too low and would give Mozart more on receipt of the work. They also agreed that the man who commissioned the work was never to be known to Mozart.

August

August was a busy month for the Mozarts. Mozart himself was working hard and there was no let up in the concerns about money. For Constanze, though, everything had changed. On 26 July, she had given birth to their son, Franz Xaver Wolfgang.

When Mozart set off, in late August, for the coronation festivities of Leopold II, Constanze went with him. Their new baby was just 1 month old, yet

the Mozarts left him behind and headed for Prague.
They did not travel completely alone, though:
Mozart's composition pupil, the 25-year-old Franz
Xaver Süssmayr, went with them. At the time, it
was quite common for composition pupils and
teachers to work jointly on pieces of music, which
would then be published in the teacher's name. In
much the same way as artists worked in "schools",
with pupils – sometimes teams of pupils –
completing works that today bear the name of just
one artist, so it was in classical music at the time.
Indeed, the practice is not unheard of today, too:
many a Hollywood movie score will credit a team
of composers, sometimes working to one
"Über-composer".

Süssmayr would almost certainly have been invited
to work on Mozart's opera, *La clemenza di Tito*.
Mozart was said to have honed it in the coach on
the way to Prague. This particular pupil's part in
Mozart's oeuvre would almost certainly have been
forgotten today, were it not for the course that this
last year of Mozart's life took. Indeed, within
months, Süssmayr would be asked to make a vital
contribution to Mozart's output – one that would
see his name live on forever.

Mozart and Constanze arrived in Prague on
28 August, just one day before the emperor and his
entourage. It is worth mentioning that Prague was
sort of the yin to Salzburg's yang. Despite Salzburg's

trade in Mozart tourism today, which brings the city hundreds of thousands of pounds every year, Mozart, as we have seen, could not wait to get out of the place. Equally, if any city truly took Mozart and his music to its heart, it could be said to be Prague. Mozart was probably more than happy, in his 35th year, to be coming back here.

September

On Sunday 4 September, some of Mozart's church music was performed at the service of the emperor's oath of allegiance, conducted by Salieri in the Cathedral of St Vitus. This was a precursor to the Monday, when *La clemenza di Tito* was premiered in the Prague National Theatre, and Tuesday, when Mozart's *Coronation Mass* was performed at the actual coronation, again at St Vitus's. Mozart's head was almost certainly full with ideas for the *Requiem* too and it would appear that, by then, the increased work rate was affecting the composer's health. He was becoming either ill or stressed or both. He had worked flat out on the composition of *La clemenza di Tito* and this huge effort had taken its toll.

The new opera was, on the whole, fairly badly received. To be fair, it was being premiered as part of the coronation celebrations and its serious, albeit suitable, subject was probably not right for its audience. It soon dropped out of the general opera repertoire and has only recently made a reappearance in the last century. It is now considered to contain some of Mozart's most beautiful operatic writing, which is not a bad achievement for something composed against the clock and partly in a coach.

Out in Prague, Mozart found time to visit the local masonic lodge, the so-called "Truth and Unity" lodge and his *Maurerfreude* – a cantata – was performed. All in all, Mozart's music was likely to have been the most played of any significant composer during the coronation period.

Back in Vienna, Mozart concerned himself with his brand new opera. It was commissioned by the impresario, Schikaneder, a fellow mason, who frequently rented out Vienna's Freihaustheater and staged productions. Mozart and Schikaneder planned it as one giant homage to the masons, and it is full of masonic images and symbols, some of them audible, some of them disguised. The three opening chords of the overture, for example, are important simply because they honour "the power of three", and are repeated, in mid-overture, as three masonic knockings – all of which would have been apparent to any fellow masons hearing the piece. Hidden, too, are various numerical references, such as groups of three and groups of 18, as well as textual references to important masonic episodes.

On 30 September, Mozart himself conducted the premiere, the first of 20 performances running into October. Ironically, the successful premiere of *The Magic Flute* coincided with a sudden upturn in fortunes for *La clemenza di Tito*, which received vigorous applause at its closing performance, on the same day. Mozart completed the orchestration of the *Clarinet Concerto in A*. Despite now being seriously overworked and suffering from depression, he also began to compose the *Requiem*. Perhaps it was around this point that the necessarily sombre subject matter of the commission began to hit him. Certainly, his depression had by now started to manifest itself in delusions that he had been poisoned. This may well have contributed to the myth surrounding his death.

There were still moments of fun and frivolity at this point of Mozart's life, though. He took Salieri to see *The Magic Flute* and his arch-rival was seemingly genuinely impressed, shouting "bravo" at several points. He also found time to play practical jokes on the opera's cast. One of the arias in *The Magic Flute* calls for a glockenspiel to be played by a singer. Usually, then as now, the glockenspiel is played *offstage* by a musician and the singer has to make it appear that he is playing a dummy instrument *onstage*. During this first ever run of *The Magic Flute*, the part was played by Schikaneder's son. One night, Mozart turned up and played the offstage instrument himself, but deliberately refused to play certain sections, or added extra bits, to fool the poor young Schikaneder:

As a joke, I played music when he was speaking. He started, looked sideways, and then clocked me. He stopped, and wouldn't carry on. I guessed what he was doing and played some more. He was forced to hit the glockenspiel, mumbling "Stop it!" Everybody laughed.

October

To add to Mozart's increasing depression, he was without Constanze, who was again at the spa in Baden. Mozart busied himself with another small cantata and then spent most of October on the *Requiem*. Accounts of this period vary wildly, but what is certain is that Mozart was getting more and more unwell. The weather in Vienna was bad, with rain, sleet and snow all making an appearance. As a result, Mozart's rheumatism was triggered and he also began to experience abdominal pains. Some musical historians claim that he put this down to having been poisoned. But whether he ever said this or, more to the point, whether the claim was actually true, is very much open to doubt. Over the years, the theories have flowed thick and fast: from malicious poisoning – by Salieri, of course – to Mozart having cooked his chops wrongly, inadvertently poisoning himself in the process.

It seems far more likely that he contracted a kidney disease and that his organs eventually failed altogether. In Mozart's own words:

I am writing this Requiem for myself.

These words are repeated so often, in so many different accounts, that it seems almost certain that Mozart probably did say them. It is, however, worth remembering that they would have been spoken by a man in pain, suffering depression and, to some extent, hallucinations.

Throughout October and part of November, Mozart completed or sketched out nearly one hundred pages of the *Requiem*. His only real moments of pleasure in this period seem to come from trips out with Constanze – now back from Baden – although these were few and far between because the weather was so bad.

November

He went to hear a lodge performance of his *Kleine Freimaurer* cantata, which apparently cheered him up no end. Both this and his occasional coach rides to the park lifted his increasingly sombre mood only temporarily and his depression soon returned. On 20 November, he felt particularly unwell and took to his bed. He was visited by his physicians, Doctors Closset and Sallaba, 7 days later.

December

In the early days of December, Mozart's condition began to rally a little, giving new hope to everyone around him. Mozart himself was still convinced of his own impending death. He was concerned enough, though, about the first performance of his *Requiem* to gather some friends from the Freihaustheater around his bedside to sing through some completed parts of the work, with Mozart himself trying to sing the alto part. When the "rehearsal" was over, a very weak Mozart pulled Süssmayr close to him and gave him detailed instructions of how to finish off the work.

Early that evening, he appeared lucid to Constanze. Later on, though, he was visited by his sister-in-law, Sophie. She was concerned enough to fetch Doctor Closset, who was at the theatre. He found Mozart feverish and burning up and applied a poultice to his forehead. Mozart lapsed into unconsciousness. The last sounds to come from his lips were an attempt to sing the one of the drum parts from the *Requiem* to Süssmayr.

Monday 5 December 1791 – if any day can claim to be "the day the music died" it is surely this one. At 5 minutes to one in the morning, Mozart's life ended. Constanze wept uncontrollably by his corpse and refused to leave his side.

133

Opera Plots

Mozart wrote more than 20 operas, of which four are extremely well known today: *The Marriage of Figaro, Don Giovanni, Così fan tutte* and *The Magic Flute*. Over the next few pages you will find our *Friendly Guide* to these four Premiership stars of the opera world. Be warned, however, that though Mozart's operas sound great when you hear them sung, the stories that they tell are by no means simple or logical. So you will need to suspend disbelief as you read their plots.

At the end of this chapter we have also listed Mozart's other operas, although if you're planning to go to the opera for the first time, here's a friendly

word of warning – we firmly recommend starting out with one of the four in our top division.

The Marriage of Figaro

Four acts. Duration: approximately two and a half hours.

First performed in the Burgtheater, Vienna, in 1786, conducted by Mozart himself.

Before we start

It is worth noting that *The Marriage of Figaro* is the sequel to *The Barber of Seville*. True, Mozart didn't compose the music for *The Barber of Seville*, but that's not really the point. A playwright called Beaumarchais wrote both stories as plays. Mozart never made an opera out of the first (Rossini did eventually), but he did make one out of the second. So, if you go to see *The Marriage of Figaro*, remember – it is actually a sequel and that it is the second outing for the main character, Figaro. In the second story, he's no longer a barber, though, and is instead a servant.

Main characters

Count and Countess	
Almaviva:	posh people
Figaro and Susanna:	servants to the posh people

Cherubino:	Count Almaviva's page
Doc Bartolo:	a doctor
Don Basilio:	a music teacher
Marcellina:	Bartolo's ex-housekeeper
Uncle Antonio:	a gardener (Susanna's uncle)
Barbarina:	Antonio's daughter

The plot

Act 1

Anyone going to a wedding needs a hat and
Susanna is going to her own wedding, so she
definitely needs one. She's going to marry Figaro.
The groom himself is not bothered with hats. He's
more concerned with beds. He spends time
measuring out the room to see what size bed will
fit. Susanna's not keen on the situation of their
bedroom because it's too close to the count, and the
count . . . well, he has something of a reputation.
She can well envisage a Ray Cooney bedroom farce.
Figaro makes suitable macho noises and then he
leaves.

Doc Bartolo enters. He's been a victim of Figaro
in the past and is always thinking about how he
will get his revenge. As is Marcellina, his one-time
housekeeper, who, apart from anything else,
wouldn't have minded marrying Figaro herself.
Marcellina and Susanna have put on starched
smiles of fake friendship and sing a duet before
Marcellina departs.

Ok, so far, so simple. Now, though, it starts to get ever so slightly complex, so you really do need your Sudoku head on. Here we go.

Cherubino, the page, walks in and begins to sing about his love for most women in general but the countess in particular. Just then, he hears the count approaching. He has no time to get out, so he hides behind a chair (where else?) and keeps quiet. The count comes in and is in the process of getting a little saucy with Susanna, Figaro's bride to be, when he hears Don Basilio, the music teacher, approaching. He decides to hide behind the chair too. Cherubino, thinking quickly, jumps up onto the chair and covers himself with a wedding dress. So – we've got Don Basilio talking to Susanna, the count behind the chair and Cherubino on the chair. All clear?

Don Basilio begins to cast general aspersions – about Susanna, about Susanna and the count, about the countess and Cherubino, about the lot. Well, if you throw enough mud, some is bound to stick! The count can't listen, and jumps out from behind the chair. He's more than a little annoyed and lets them in on the reason *why* . . . he was going to sack Cherubino, anyway! (Remember, Cherubino's on the chair, under a dress.) It turns out that the count was visiting a certain young woman named Barbarina the other day and guess what happened? When the count innocently lifted the cover of the tablecloth, who was under the table but Cherubino? As if to demonstrate, he feigns pulling up the tablecloth with . . . let's see, the wedding dress on the chair. Lo and behold, who is underneath again, but Cherubino? Once is unfortunate, twice is careless. The count isn't best pleased, not least because Cherubino must have heard everything.

Figaro now comes back in with a group of peasants. He strews flowers all over the place. Has he gone slightly poppyloo? No, this is merely a precursor to asking the count to attend his and Susanna's wedding. The count eventually agrees, but then pulls Cherubino aside. He tells him that he's going to sign him up into the army to teach him a lesson. Figaro warns Cherubino that the life of a soldier is pretty tough and his days of wild oats, and, more to the point, their sowing, are now over. That last bit comes across in one of the most famous songs in the opera, *"Non più andrai"* (which translates, very loosely indeed, as "You can't go round sowing your wild oats any longer!").

Act 2

The countess is firmly of the belief that the count doesn't love her. In fact, she believes this so much, she sings a song about it, *"Porgi amor"*. Susanna comes in and unwisely lets the countess know that her husband, the count, fancies her. This was probably not the best decision she made that day. Then, Cherubino walks in and declares his

undying, if rather naïve, love for the countess – "*Voi che sapete*" (or "Now, you're a woman of the world"). Hang on a mo, thinks Susanna: the count was getting saucy with me earlier, asking to meet me and what have you. Between them, Susannah and the countess are really out for the count. They decide that they'll say yes to an assignation with the count, but instead of Susanna going, they'll dress Cherubino up as a girl and send him. Of course – it's the most obvious thing to do. They lock the door and get to work, tarting up Cherubino – putting a dress on him, doing his nails, filling his handbag with dozens of useless items. But then, the count is heard approaching. (Rule 1 of opera: always make yourself heard "approaching".) Cherubino is locked into an inner room, while Susanna hides in an alcove.

The count is suspicious. Why was the door locked? Why is the inner room door locked? The countess says Susanna is in there. In disbelief, he carts the countess off with him to fetch tools to break open the door. While he's gone, Susanna unlocks the inner room, lets Cherubino out the window and then locks herself in. When the count returns with his battering ram, the countess thinks she's about to be found out and confesses that it's actually Cherubino in there. The door is then forced and out comes . . . of course, Susanna. The count is surprised. The countess is flabbergasted. She says her confession was obtained under duress and was just to make him feel bad. The count apologizes for doubting her.

Just then, Antonio, the slightly merry gardener, comes in. Although he's a bit "the worse for wear" (and it's only early in the day) he's come to complain. There he was, minding his own business, when someone jumped out of the countess's window and landed on top of him. Figaro, who's now on the scene himself, says it was him. Antonio then says, whoever it was, they dropped Cherubino's call-up papers for army. Figaro still maintains it was him. At this point, just when you thought it couldn't get any dafter, Marcellina, Doc Bartolo and Don Basilio walk in and make a rather amazing claim: that Figaro can't marry Susanna. He is legally obliged to marry Marcellina to make up for a bad debt. Thank goodness the curtain comes down.

Act 3

Susanna and the count sing a song in which they arrange to meet in the garden. But the count is suspicious and not convinced, especially when he overhears Susanna and Figaro talking, and gets just a little bit annoyed.

Marcellina, Doc Bartolo and the count's lawyer all appear to doorstep Figaro. Marry Marcellina, or else, is their message. Figaro says he can't because he's actually of noble birth and, as such, would need the permission of his folks to marry. To prove he's

nobly born, he does two things. First, he tells them he once had some nice clothes. Mmm – don't think it would stand up in court. Second, he's got a strange, "noble" birthmark on his arm, look! As soon as he reveals it, Marcellina squeals and nearly falls over. Why? Because that's an inherited birthmark – Figaro is her son. What's more, Doc Bartolo is Figaro's dad.

Everyone sings about how weird it all is. Figaro and his new-found mum, Marcellina, embrace. Just as they do, Susanna enters, and jumps to the wrong conclusions. (Rule 2 of opera: if a conclusion is to be jumped to, it should be a wrong one.) Susanna gives Figaro a slap, until Marcellina explains that he's her son. Oh, well, that's all right then.

Cue the countess, who's been feeling a little left out. She sings a song about … yes, same as before, really: "*Dove sono. . .*" ("Where have all the good times gone?"). She makes her mind up to teach the count a lesson and tells Susanna to write him a letter. She dictates the letter in a cute little song, where she sings a line and Susanna repeats it ("*The Letter Song*", or "*Letter Duet*").

Some peasant girls enter again – having enjoyed it so much the first time – although one of them is actually a cross-dressing Cherubino (who appears to be enjoying his new outfit just a little too much). Antonio, the slightly slewed gardener, unmasks him

(or should that be defrocks him?) and he's about to
feel the full force of the count's wrath when . . . ?
Well, when Barbarina mentions that he promised
her she could have anything when he was . . . well,
when he was . . . in the "promising anything" mood.
She says she wants Cherubino spared as her
"anything" and the count reluctantly agrees, keen for
her not to reveal all about their previous dalliances.

Figaro announces that the wedding ceremony and
general merrymaking are about to begin. It's to be
a double wedding, though: not just Figaro and
Susannah, but also, belatedly, Marcellina and Doc
Bartolo. A crowd gathers. During a frolicsome
fandango, Susanna slips the dictated letter into the
count's pocket, asking for a cheeky rendezvous, that
night. Little does he know, though, it won't be
Susanna turning up. It won't even be his cross-
dressing page. It will be the countess herself, in
Susanna's cloak. Now that will put the cat among
the pigeons.

Act 4
Ok, this is a complicated one, so hang on to your
hats. The scene is set for the rendezvous to end all
rendezvous. The count has sent Barbarina to
Susanna, complete with her pin that was stuck onto
the original letter. Figaro meets her looking for the
pin that she has dropped and "realizes" that his
beloved Susanna has a love tryst arranged with the
count. Of course, he doesn't know that it isn't going

to be Susanna at all, so he gathers Doc Bartolo and Don Basilio to join him in witnessing his new wife's unfaithfulness. They retire to the wings to watch.

Susanna and the countess enter, dressed as each other. Susanna sings of looking forward to love, knowing that the jealous Fig is watching. Now here's where the fun starts. As well as the count and "Susanna", Cherubino has arranged to meet Barbarina. When Cherubino sees the countess dressed as Susanna (and thinking it Susanna) he tries to kiss her. (So Barbarina didn't last long, then.) The count steps in, though, and it's he who gets kissed. The count then tries to slap Cherubino in disgust, but that's when Figaro steps in and it's *he* who gets slapped.

Figaro decides to pay the count back and so starts to reveal the whole plot to the countess – or, at least, to the woman he thinks is the countess, but is, in fact, his own wife, Susanna. Susanna forgets to disguise her voice and Figaro soon realizes who he's talking to. So he, too, decides to have a little fun by declaring mad, passionate love to her – supposedly the countess – knowing full well it's his wife. Susanna is more than a little miffed that Figaro is declaring his love for the woman that she thinks he thinks is the countess. She soon realizes, though, but then the two of them – Figaro and Susanna – continue with the deception together, just to annoy the count, who is apoplectic at the sight of them snogging. The count is on the verge of having them both run through, when the real countess comes forward and reveals that Figaro is, in fact, kissing Susanna. Thank goodness for that. The count is laid low with shame on all . . . er, counts. The countess, though, forgives him and they all indulge in general merrymaking as the curtain closes.

Don Giovanni

Two acts. Duration: approximately two and a half hours.

First performed in the National Theatre, Prague, in 1787.

Before we start

Mozart generally wrote two types of opera: comic or serious. *Don Giovanni*, though, was positioned somewhere in between, and is neither one genre nor the other – a bit like *Cold Feet*. He wrote the work for the opera house in Prague, a city that seemed to love both him and his music. In continental Europe, it is known as *Don Juan*, the story on which it is based, but in England we have kept with the Italian version of the title.

Main characters

Don Giovanni: an amoral nobleman
Leporello: his servant

Donna Elvira:	a woman scorned by Don G
Don Ottavio:	Don G's friend
Donna Anna:	Ottavio's fiancée
The Commendatore:	Donna Anna's dad
Zerlina and Masetto:	peasant girl and boy, betrothed
Donna Elvira's maid:	who doesn't get to say much. In fact, nothing at all

random peasants
and spooky sorts

The plot

Act 1

The opera opens at the house of Donna Anna. Outside, Leporello is moaning about his life as more or less a henchman of Don Giovanni. Inside, the man himself is attempting to have his wicked way with Donna Anna, from behind the relative safety of a mask. The Commendatore, Donna Anna's father, comes in and discovers what's going on. He challenges Don Giovanni and, in the fight that follows, is killed. Don Giovanni and Leporello escape. Donna Anna finds her father dead and persuades her fiancée, Don Ottavio, to swear to hunt down whoever did it. Unfortunately, because of his mask, she doesn't know who it was.

Later, in the street, Don Giovanni and Leporello come across a woman who is bemoaning her fate as a scorned lover. Don Giovanni begins to "comfort"

her, but soon realizes that it's his old flame, Donna Elvira, and quickly scarpers, leaving Leporello, thoughtfully, to recount a catalogue of his conquests (known as the *"Catalogue Aria"*).

Nearby, in a little village, it's all about to happen again. Masetto and Zerlina are about to get hitched when the lascivious Don Giovanni moves in. He gets Leporello to whisk Masetto away and starts giving it the "Leslie Phillips" with Zerlina: "So what star sign are you . . . ooh, lovely hands . . . look, they just fit mine . . . oh, Zerlina, that was my mother's name." This comes out in an aria called *"Là ci darem la mano"*. Just as he's about to succeed, Elvira turns up and rains on his parade. She warns the poor girl and ferries her to safety. Cue Donna Anna and Don Ottavio, to join everyone in an "isn't Don Giovanni awful" song. Elvira tries to tell the two lovers that Don Giovanni is a nasty piece of work, but he counters with claims that she's deranged. Crucially, though, Donna Anna recognizes his voice as the "one who tried to rob me of my honour" and Don Ottavio gets the message. Are Don Giovanni's days numbered?

Don Giovanni invites everyone back to his place for a party and who knows what else. This is called the *"Champagne Aria"*. Don Giovanni scoots and Masetto enters. He's a little miffed with Zerlina for indulging the flirting Don Giovanni but, once she's sung to him, she has him round her tiny digit.

Don Giovanni returns with cries of "Everyone back to my gaff", and unwittingly invites the masked figures of Donna Anna, Don Ottavio and Donna Elvira, who say a small prayer for everything to go right.

At the party, while everyone's dancing, Don Giovanni makes another pass at Zerlina. This time, Zerlina kicks and screams and Don Giovanni covers himself by pretending it was Leporello who was the villain. Thanks, boss. But, as the curtain closes, Donna Anna, Don Ottavio and Donna Elvira all throw off their masks and denounce him. Surely the game is up? We'll find out after the interval.

Act 2

So, is the game up? Well, apparently not. (Rule 3 of opera: when the game looks as though it's up, it's never *actually* up.) As the curtain rises, Don Giovanni is working the charm on Donna Elvira's maid, who doesn't say much in return. In fact, nothing. He's switched cloaks with Leporello (Rule 4 of opera: have cloak, will switch) and sent his servant off to keep Donna Elvira busy, leaving him free to pursue La Silenta, complete with mandolin.

Masetto turns up to kill Don Giovanni, but he has Leporello's cloak on and is, clearly, totally unidentifiable. Somehow, too, he manages to give Masetto a bit of a slap when he's least expecting it, and it's left to Zerlina to comfort the ailing if hapless Masetto.

Meanwhile, Leporello-disguised-as-Don-Giovanni and Donna Elvira bump into Zerlina and Masetto, and – *quelle surprise* – Donna Anna and Don Ottavio. They all think Leporello is Don Giovanni and go for him, but, amazingly, Donna Elvira defends him. Before long, though, Leporello spills the beans and lets everyone in on the fact that this cloak is not his and he's not Don Giovanni. All go their separate ways.

The action cuts to a cemetery. Don Giovanni and Leporello come across the statue of the dearly departed Commendatore, whom Don Giovanni killed. Now, hold on to your coat-tails for this bit. The statue . . . speaks. It's pretty annoyed and has a go at Don Giovanni. Leporello is scared stiff, but Don Giovanni doesn't seem to care. In fact, he invites him back for dinner.

The scene changes again to Don Giovanni dining at home. He has his own house band playing for him. Leporello is serving him. All is right with his world, except when Donna Elvira runs in and looks like she's seen a ghost. Leporello goes to look and is terrified, again. It is the statue, walking spookily towards the house, on his way to dine with Don Giovanni. It comes into the house and pulls the defiant Don Giovanni down with it into

the flames of hell, as a chorus of invisible spooks sings along.

At last, all the others enter, wanting to kill Don Giovanni. Leporello explains they are too late. Amazingly, they buy his story that Don Giovanni "was dragged down into hell by a cemetery statue" and are pacified. All vow to do their own thing – Donna Anna will marry Don Ottavio, but in a year's time (it's called playing hard to get, isn't it?); Zerlina and Masetto are going home to eat; Leporello is going to get a new boss; and Donna Elvira, well, she's going to join a convent. They all face the audience and tell them to learn the lesson of . . . Don Giovanni. It's all a bit "Scooby-Doo" at the end, really. You can almost hear the voice of Don Giovanni saying: "And I'd have done it, if it hadn't been for those pesky kids."

Così fan tutte

Two acts. Duration: approximately three hours.

First performed in the Burgtheater, Vienna, in 1790, again conducted by Mozart himself.

Before we start

Let's talk about the title. It's a weird one, so let's strip it down. **Così** means "thus", "in this way" or "like this"; **fan** means "do"; so far, so good. It's the last word that needs a little finessing, though. In Italian, words come in genders: some words are masculine, some are feminine. **Tutte** is the feminine version of the Italian word for "all". So, even though there is no word for "woman" or "women" in this opera title, it has to be translated as something like "Thus do all (women)". Mmm. See? Slightly tricky. People often go for translations such as "All women do it" or "That's what all women do". It might give you a better idea of what the opera's about (and save everyone an awful lot of time) if it went by the subtitle Mozart gave it – "The School for Lovers". It's a Ronseal sort of title: it does what it says on the tin. Anyway, this opera is one huge, light romp, removed from the world of bedroom farce purely by the fact that Mozart reserved some of his most sublime music for it.

Main characters

Ferrando:	an officer and a gentleman, in love with . . .
Dorabella:	a young lady of Ferrara
Guglielmo:	also an officer and a gentleman and in love with . . .
Fiordiligi:	sister of Dorabella
Don Alfonso:	an ageing philosopher
Despina:	the maid

Plus various serfs, soldiers, servants, and other lowlife. There are even musicians

The plot

Act 1

Ferrando and Guglielmo are down the local, enthusing about their respective girlfriends, Dorabella and Fiordiligi. Ferrando says that Dorabella loves him unequivocally and would never be unfaithful to him. Guglielmo says the same about Fiordiligi. Don Alfonso, the wise old philosopher, begs to differ, which somewhat annoys the two dashing blades. Don Alfonso challenges them and they bet on their girlfriends' honour in the face of anything that Don Alfonso can throw at them. They even discuss what they are going to do with the money, once they have fleeced Don Alfonso.

At the girls' house, Dorabella and Fiordiligi are gazing adoringly and somewhat pathetically at pictures of their two hunks. The door bursts open. It's Don Alfonso, who asks them if they want the good news or the bad news. They take the bad news – that Ferrando and Guglielmo have been called up by the army and have to go away. What's the good news? Well, you can both see them off. The men enter and the two pairs of lovers sing about undying love. The officers march off with the girls (and Don Alfonso) wishing them a good trip, in one of the best songs in this or any opera: *"Soave sia il vento"* – which translates very loosely indeed as something like "May the wind be gentle but don't forget to write". And they're gone. Or are they?

Elsewhere in the house, Despina, the maid, is complaining about her work. She thinks Dorabella and Fiordiligi live the life of Riley and can't believe it when she hears them nagging on about how unhappy they are. The sisters say they can't live without their blokes. Despina replies with something along the lines of "Whatever! Lighten up!" The sisters leave and Don Alfonso enters.

Don Alfonso asks Despina if she'd like to make some extra money. All she has to do is introduce his two friends to Dorabella and Fiordiligi. His two friends, incidentally, are Ferrando and Guglielmo, disguised as Albanians. Despina gets the "Albanians" together with the sisters. In a group song, Dorabella and Fiordiligi are disgusted at being approached. Fiordiligi, in particular, says she will never waver in her devotion – a moving song called *"Come scoglio"*.

Ferrando talks up the boys' merits, which, among other things, include the fact that they both have big noses. Don't ask us. The girls leave – well, there was no reason to mention big noses – and the boys are over the moon. The money is as good as spent. Don Alfonso, however, still doesn't think so. Ferrando, just to show his feminine side, then sings a song about how in love he is, called *"Un' aura amorosa"* – an aura of love.

There's no time to dawdle, though. Don Alfonso
and Despina have already hatched the next part of
the plan. Now, if you feel you have already
suspended your disbelief, maybe prepare to hire a
crane, because it's about to need suspending further.
(Rule 5 of opera: why simply suspend disbelief
when you can kill it completely and then kick it
while it's down?)

Ferrando and Guglielmo (as Albanians, remember)
catch up with the sisters and pretend to take poison.
They both drop lifeless to the floor so Don Alfonso
and Despina run out "to get a doctor". While they
are gone, it's clear that the girls have been more
than a little impressed by their amazing act of
undying (or should that be dying) love. The boys,
although fake dead, comment now and then, when
the girls are not looking.

Don Alfonso returns with the doctor (who is, of
course, Despina with a moustache). Doc Despina
recites all manner of bogus Latin and then produces
a huge magnet, which s/he passes over the boys'
corpses, bringing them back to life. The boys,
clearly reinvigorated by their magnetic experience,
surprise the girls by asking for a kiss. Thankfully,
the curtain closes before it all gets out of hand.

Act 2

The second act starts with Despina egging her
mistresses on, trying to get them to flirt a little.

When she's gone, Dorabella and Fiordiligi decide they will do, after all. Dorabella chooses Albanian Guglielmo, and Fiordiligi chooses Albanian Ferrando – so, in fact, they've chosen each other's lovers. This could be fun.

Out in the garden, Ferrando and Guglielmo have laid on musicians to play for the girls. When Dorabella and Fiordiligi arrive, the boys pretend to be shy, so Don Alfonso and Despina take them through a little courtship ritual song, before making themselves scarce. At first, the four talk about the weather – always a good start. Then things begin to hot up. While Ferrando leads Fiordiligi off, Guglielmo persuades Dorabella to swap lockets – she gets a heart shape one from him, while he gets a miniature picture of Ferrando! Just what will he have to say about that?

Meanwhile, Fiordiligi and Ferrando are not quite at the same level. She will not take things further, despite admitting to herself that she seems to have feelings for her Albanian.

The two boys meet up. Ferrando can happily report that Fiordiligi has not budged, but Guglielmo, sadly, shows him the locket that Dorabella was willing to exchange in return for "his heart". Guglielmo sings a song about women being generally inconsistent, while Ferrando sings of still being madly in love, despite what has happened.

Back at the girls' place, Dorabella is happy, but Fiordiligi is worried. She decides that they must save their honour. How to do this, remembering that this is opera? Of course – they should dress up in the soldiers' uniforms that Guglielmo and Ferrando left behind. What else? Alas, Ferrando enters and steps up his wooing – he's at Charm Central, and it appears to be Fiordiligi's undoing. In the end, she succumbs.

It's at this point that Guglielmo, Ferrando and Don Alfonso sing that women will always behave like this: *"Così fan tutte"*, of course.

The action cuts to a room set for a party – a wedding party. The girls are to marry their Albanians. Well, they don't waste time in opera. The boys and the girls sing a cute quartet, interspersed with some rather bitter asides from Albanian Guglielmo. Poor lad – that'll teach him to bet. The notary arrives to conduct the wedding (of course, it's Despina in an even bigger moustache than before). Just as the marriage contract is about to be signed, though, soldiers are heard singing outside. Albanian Ferrando and Albanian Guglielmo run off and return as . . . plain old Ferrando and Guglielmo. They "spot" the marriage contract; they "spot" the notary, who quickly reveals herself to be Despina in a large moustache. The girls blush, whisper something about entrapment and admit they were planning a wedding – but only a small one.

The men shock the girls by revealing it was their plot, all along, and everyone agrees to kiss and make up. Don Alfonso has won his bet, the girls are apparently "chastened" and they all live happily ever after.

The Magic Flute

Two acts. Duration: approximately two hours and 40 minutes.

First performed in the Theater auf der Wieden, Vienna, in 1791.

Before we start

It is often said that *The Magic Flute* is Mozart's version of a panto – silly, camp in places and with a great stage baddie to boo and hiss (the Queen of the Night). The plot is bizarre, too, even by opera standards.

Main characters

The Queen of the Night:	you wouldn't want to meet her in a dark alley
Three ladies:	they work for the queen
Pamina:	the queen's daughter
Tamino:	a prince
Papageno:	a birdcatcher

Papagena: the bird that the
                                   birdcatcher catches

Plus an assortment of priests, slaves and the like

The plot

Act 1

Prince Tamino is knocked unconscious by
a monster, which is killed by three mysterious ladies,
who quite fancy him. On waking, he meets
a mischievous birdcatcher (is that really a job?)
called Papageno. The three ladies padlock Papageno's
mouth for lying and show Tamino a picture of a
beautiful girl, the daughter of the queen. They tell
him that she is a prisoner of nasty Sarastro and he
decides he will free her. Scene change.

Pamina, the girl in the picture, is receiving the
unwanted attentions of Sarastro's number two,
Monostatos. Papageno sees him off, much to
Pamina's delight. Scene change again.

Tamino tries to gain entry into three temples, but
fails twice. At the third attempt, a speaker emerges
and tells him that Sarastro is no baddie after all, but
that the Queen of the Night *is*. Tamino sings and
plays his magic flute (yes, *the* magic flute) and
soothes a few savage beasts in the process. He
scarpers, stage right, though, when he hears
Papageno's panpipe (*not* the magic flute). In true
panto style, Papageno enters stage left, with Pamina.

When Monostatos enters and things look like turning ugly, Papageno plays his magic chimes (there's a lot of it about – magic, that is) and Monostatos dances off. Sarastro now enters, amidst huge pomp. Pamina and Papageno explain what had been going on so, when Monostatos arrives, dragging our hero Tamino, he gets short shrift and is sent off, with ear now home to flea. Oh, and a good flogging. Well, this is before the corporal punishment ban. Sarastro also asks Papageno and Tamino to prove themselves. Exciting. End of Act 1. Time for a chunky choc-ice.

Act 2

Tamino and Papageno's ordeals kick off. They are left alone, but who should show up but the three ladies, who try to persuade them to give it all up and nip off for a cheeky cappuccino. Both stay shtoom, and so Sarastro appears to tell them they have passed test number one. Scene change.

Pamina is asleep. The sleazy Monostatos slimes up to her, intent on who knows what, but is forced back by the Queen of the Night – he must be getting used to this by now. The evil queen slings Pam a dagger and asks her to kill Sarastro. Slimeball Monostatos slithers up to Pam, again, and says he'll tell all – about the dagger – to Sarastro, if she doesn't . . . you know! Sarastro arrives not a moment too soon and dispatches Monostatos – now with veritable colony of insects in aural canal. Scene change.

Papageno meets his future love, Papagena, who is, shall we say, mature in years and displeasing of phizog. Papageno is not exactly impressed. Meanwhile, Pamina has hooked up with Tamino, but he's still on his sponsored silence and she's heartbroken that he won't speak to her. Sarastro appears to tell Pam and Tam to say what could be their final goodbye. Papageno is forced to swear undying love to the somewhat facially challenged crone. When he does – PUFF! – she's transformed into the young and beautiful Papagena, although they can't be together until Pap has proved himself.

Tamino is then led off for his final ordeals – fire and water. With Pamina in tow, he passes with flying colours, dropping only a few points for not using his mirror. Papageno is also cheered up when he is allowed to be with Papagena. Just to round things off, Sarastro vanquishes the Queen of the Night and her three ladies in a huge flood of bright, do-gooding light. All are happy, the opera is over and it's time to join the mad rush to get your coat from the cloakroom.

And the rest of Mozart's operas:
Apollo et Hyacinthus seu Hyacinthi Metamorphosis
Bastien und Bastienne
La finta semplice (The Make-believe Simpleton)
Mitridate, rè di Ponto
Ascanio in Alba
Il sogno di Scipione (Scipio's Dream)

Lucio Silla

La finta giardiniera (The Make-believe Gardener)

Il rè pastore (The Shepherd King)

Thamos, König in Ägypten

Zaide

Idomeneo, rè di Creta

Die Entführung aus dem Serail (The Abduction from the Harem)

L'oca del Cairo (The Cairo Goose)

Lo sposo deluso, ossia la rivalità di tre donne per un solo amante (The Deluded Bridegroom, or the Rivalry of Three Women for the Same Lover)

Der Schauspieldirektor (The Impresario)

La clemenza di Tito (The Clemency of Titus)

Have a Listen Yourself

Every year, our listeners vote for their favourite three pieces of music in the Classic FM Hall of Fame. Here, we have gathered together a list of Mozart's Top 20 works, as voted by Classic FM listeners.

You will find excerpts of each of these pieces on the CD that accompanies this book. Hopefully, these tasty morsels will whet your appetite for listening to more of the great man's music. We have deliberately chosen all of the excerpts from full-length CDs on the Naxos label. All Naxos discs are released at a budget price and represent excellent value for money,

so you will quickly be able to build up a relatively inexpensive collection of Mozart's greatest hits.

1 *Clarinet Concerto in A*

Written shortly before Mozart died, this piece has always been a firm favourite. It was used to particularly good effect in the film *Out of Africa*. Mozart composed the piece for his good friend, Anton Stadler, whose playing he admired enormously. It's worth remembering that in Mozart's day, the clarinet only had six keys, compared with the modern instrument's 20. So playing this piece back then required particular dexterity.

CD Track 1 is an excerpt from the 2nd movement, taken from Naxos 8.550345.

If you enjoy this, then try Mozart's *Bassoon Concerto* (also on Naxos 8.550345).

2 *Requiem*

One of the greatest requiems ever written. Mozart didn't manage to finish this piece. In fact, it was still being rehearsed by his bedside the night before he died. It was as if the great man were writing his own tribute to himself. It was commissioned by an anonymous messenger working on behalf of Count von Walsegg. The count planned to pretend that he had written the piece, but the terrible effect the cloak-and-dagger commissioning process had on Mozart's state of mind shouldn't be underestimated.

CD Track 2 is "*Kyrie*", taken from Naxos 8.550235.

If you enjoy this, then try Mozart's *Mass in C, The Coronation Mass* (Naxos 8.550495).

3 *Piano Concerto No. 21 in C*

The strange case of a piece of music making a film famous, rather than the other way around. This work is known as the *Elvira Madigan* after it was used in a Swedish film. That movie is long since forgotten by all but the keenest of film buffs. But Mozart's music very definitely lives on, with this work being a particularly big crowd pleaser in concert halls.

CD Track 3 is an excerpt from the extraordinarily beautiful 2nd movement, taken from Naxos 8.550202.

If you enjoy this, then try Mozart's *Piano Concerto No. 27*, which was the last piano concerto he ever wrote (Naxos 8.550203).

4 *The Magic Flute*

This opera can be enjoyed and understood on two levels. On the first level, it is a comedy romp full of

pantomime-style caricatures and on the other level, it is packed full of references to Mozart's freemasonry. Over the years, more academic analysis has probably been given to the second level than the first, but above all, this opera is fun. (For the full plot, see pages 157–60.)

CD Track 4 is an excerpt from "*Pa-pa-pa*", a duet between Papageno and Papagena, taken from Naxos 8.660030-31.

If you enjoy this, then try Mozart's *Così fan tutte* (Naxos 8.660008-10).

5 *The Marriage of Figaro*

As soon as this opera was first performed in 1786, Mozart knew that he had a hit on his hands. It's very easy to see going to the opera as a very serious or worthy way of spending an evening, but this opera was written to be enjoyed. It's a great example of highly populist 18th-century entertainment, although behind the jollity, there are some serious messages. (For the full plot, see pages 136–45.)

CD Track 5 is an excerpt from the opera's overture, which is among the most famous ever written for any opera. It is taken from Naxos 8.554172.

If you enjoy this, then try Mozart's *Don Giovanni* (Naxos 8.660080-82).

6 *Ave verum corpus*

Written just months before Mozart died, this very beautiful sacred song has an intense poignancy to it. It is barely three minutes long, but don't underestimate the power of this work just because it's among the shortest of Mozart's most famous pieces.

CD Track 6 is taken from Naxos 8.550495.

If you enjoy this, then try Mozart's *Kyrie in D minor* (Naxos 8.554421).

7 *"Laudate Dominum"*

Another of Mozart's religious works, here he has set the words of Psalm 116 to music. *"Laudate Dominum"* is part of his *Solemn Vespers of a Confessor*, which were composed to be sung in Salzburg Cathedral.

CD Track 7 is an excerpt, taken from Naxos 8.550495.

If you enjoy this, then try Mozart's *Vesperae de Dominica (Sunday Vespers)* (Naxos 8.554158).

8 *Eine kleine Nachtmusik*

One of the best known of all Mozart's compositions, its correct title is *Serenade No.13 in G*. The epithet *Eine kleine Nachtmusik* translates as "a little night music". This would have been written for a gathering of noblemen and would have been presented as part of the evening's entertainment. He wrote this piece while he was in the middle of composing his opera *Don Giovanni*. Mozart was never one for starting and finishing one piece of music at a time and would often have many different pieces on the go at the same time – some nearing completion and some only rough sketches of musical phrases that would later be turned into masterpieces.

CD Track 8 is an excerpt from the first movement, which is one of the most famous tunes from this four-movement work. It is taken from Naxos 8.550026.

If you enjoy this, then try Mozart's *Serenade No. 10 in B Flat for 13 Wind Instruments – "Gran partita"* (Naxos 8.550060).

9 *Flute and Harp Concerto*

Written for the daughter of one of his Parisian patrons, who was a fine flautist, the last movement

of this concerto almost seems to be a good-natured
battle between the flute and the harp, as each
attempts to better the other with an ever
more melodic tune.

CD Track 9 is an excerpt from the third
movement, taken from Naxos 8.557011.

If you enjoy this, then try Mozart's *Violin Concerto
No. 5* (Naxos 8.550293).

10 *Così fan tutte*

Mozart's fellow great composers, Beethoven and
Wagner, were rather disparaging about this opera,
but for many critics this is in fact his greatest opera.
In common with *The Marriage of Figaro* and *Don
Giovanni*, the libretto was composed by Lorenzo da
Ponte. These three massive hits underline Mozart
and da Ponte's place as one of the most enduring
double acts anywhere in operatic history. (For the
full plot, see pages 150–7.)

CD Track 10 is an excerpt from the aria "*Soave sia
il vento*", which must surely be among the most
beautiful in any opera. It is taken from Naxos
8.660008-10.

If you enjoy this, then try Mozart's *The Marriage of
Figaro* (Naxos 8.660102-04).

11 *Clarinet Quintet in A*

Many music lovers believe that Mozart was at his best when writing for the clarinet. His close friendship with Anton Stadler meant that he always knew that whatever he wrote for this instrument, no matter how intricate, there would also be a musician close by who could bring his music to life. The *Clarinet Quintet* has been overshadowed to an extent by the success of the *Clarinet Concerto*, but it deserves to be heard by the widest possible audience.

CD Track 11 is an excerpt from the wonderful second movement, taken from Naxos 8.550390.

If you enjoy this, then try Mozart's *Oboe Quartet* (Naxos 8.555913).

12 *Piano Concerto No. 23 in A*

Rather than being a big bold piano concerto, this is a far more gentle affair. It begins with a bright and optimistic first movement, followed by an emotionally charged second movement, before the pace quickens in the last movement, when we hear a lot from the woodwind section of the orchestra.

CD Track 12 is an excerpt from the opening movement, taken from Naxos 8.550204.

If you enjoy this, then try Mozart's *Piano Concerto No. 24*, which was written at the same time as his *Piano Concerto No. 23* at the beginning of 1786 (Naxos 8.550204).

13 *Symphony No. 40 in G minor*

Mozart's *Symphonies Nos. 39, 40* and *41* were all written in less than 2 months, which is an astounding achievement. As you might expect, the urgent need for a cash injection was behind this flurry of composition. Sadly for Mozart, he didn't raise the money that he needed – but he did leave us with three of the finest symphonies he wrote. The middle symphony has a sadness about it, but despite that feeling of melancholy, it has steadfastly remained the most popular of all of his symphonies among Classic FM listeners.

CD Track 13 is an excerpt from the very beginning of the first movement, taken from Naxos 8.550299.

If you enjoy this, then try Mozart's *Symphony No. 29*, which is a far brighter and cheerier work and which, coincidentally, was written when he was actually 29 years old (Naxos 8.550119).

14 *Piano Concerto No. 20 in D minor*

If Mozart's *Symphony No. 40* is his "darker" symphony, then this work performs the same function among his piano concertos. Usually, they have an upbeat feel to them, but this one starts in a rather menacing, stormy way. The final movement is particularly highly charged – it's as if you can hear a battle between optimism and pessimism going on in the music. Eventually though, the feeling that the glass is half-full, rather than half-empty, wins through.

CD Track 14 is an excerpt from the third movement, taken from Naxos 8.550201.

If you enjoy this, then try Mozart's *Piano Sonata No. 11*, which includes the well-known Turkish-themed final movement (Naxos 8.550258).

15 *Symphony No. 41 in C ("Jupiter")*

This is the final symphony that Mozart wrote. It's not entirely clear how this piece came by its nickname, but it is known to everyone as the "Jupiter". It could be because the music has an imperial feeling to it – just as you would expect the king of the gods to sound. Mozart's son said it was given its sobriquet by an impresario called

Johann Salomon, who was the co-founder of the Philharmonic Society of London. Records from a concert given by the Society in March 1821 show that the nickname was being used by then.

CD Track 15 is an excerpt from the first movement, taken from Naxos 8.550299.

If you enjoy this, then try Mozart's *Symphony No. 39* (Naxos 8.550186).

16 *Don Giovanni*

An enthralling mixture of bedroom farce and deep tragedy, this opera is packed full of big tunes including the "*Catalogue Aria*", in which we hear about Don Giovanni's long list of sexual conquests in full, and "*Là ci darem la mano*", where the testosterone-driven leading man woos a peasant girl. (For the full plot, see pages 145–50.)

CD Track 16 is an excerpt from the opera's overture, which, legend has it, was written by Mozart in the early hours of the morning on the very day that the opera was due to receive its premiere. There is no way you would know that from listening to it, though. It is taken from Naxos 8.660080-82.

If you enjoy this, then try Mozart's *The Magic Flute* (Naxos 8.660030-31).

17 *Horn Concerto No. 2 in E♭*

Mozart wrote five horn concertos during his life and this makes it hard to believe that when he was a small boy, he was absolutely terrified of the instrument. One musician described how, when he blew his horn in Wolfgang's direction, the colour instantly drained out of the boy's cheeks. The horn player seriously thought the young Mozart would have suffered a fit had he not stopped playing.

CD Track 17 is an excerpt from the third movement, taken from Naxos 8.553592.

If you enjoy this, then try Mozart's *Horn Concerto No. 4* (also on Naxos 8.553592).

18 *Exsultate, jubilate*

Lasting around a quarter of an hour, this piece was written to be sung in a church. These days, it is performed by a soprano, but Mozart didn't actually write it for a soprano at all. Instead, he had the castrato, Venanzio Rauzzini in mind to perform it. This is an uplifting work throughout and the last of the three movements is notable because Mozart chooses to set only one word to music for its duration: "Alleluia".

CD Track 18 is an excerpt from the final movement, taken from Naxos 8.550495.

If you enjoy this, then try Mozart's *Mass No. 18 in C minor ("The Great Mass")* (Naxos 8.554421).

19 Mass No. 18 in C minor ("The Great Mass")

Usually Mozart wrote his church music because of a specific commission. In this case, though, he wrote the work for another reason altogether. He promised to write a mass in gratitude if his wife Constanze became well again after being dangerously ill. She did get better and this is the result. He may well have been grateful, but it's still worth noting that he never actually got around to finishing the whole work.

CD Track 19 is the "*Gloria*", which is one of the bits he did write, taken from Naxos 8.554421.

If you enjoy this, then try Mozart's *Coronation Mass* (Naxos 8.550495).

20 Sinfonia Concertante for Violin, Viola and Orchestra

This is one of two *sinfonie concertanti* that Mozart wrote. These are very similar to concertos, but the solo players (in this case, the violin and viola) work more closely with the rest of the orchestra, rather than starring on their own.

It's quite possible that Michael Haydn, the brother of Mozart's great friend, Joseph Haydn, played the viola in the original performances. In the slow second movement, both the violin and viola have big solo parts before they become linked together in the music.

CD Track 20 is an excerpt from the upbeat third movement. It's taken from Naxos 8.550332.

If you enjoy this, then try Mozart's *Sinfonia Concertante for Oboe, Clarinet, Horn, Bassoon and Orchestra* (Naxos 8.550159).

09

Mozart's Movie Music

Mozart's music has proved to be a popular choice for film directors the world over. This is by no means an exhaustive list of movies that include music he composed, but it does include one or two surprises. *Eine kleine Nachtmusik* appears more times in our list than any other work, but the *Requiem*, the *Clarinet Concerto* and the Overture to *The Marriage of Figaro* are also frequently heard accompanying the hits of the silver screen.

So the chances are that you may well have been hearing Mozart's music while you were at the

cinema, without even realizing it. Make sure that you listen out for his masterpieces when you next rent that DVD – you can never quite be certain where his tunes are going to turn up next.

Amadeus

Before we start going through other movies, this film deserves a section all of its own. Released in 1984 and directed by Milos Forman, it was based on the 1979 stage play of the same name, by Peter Shaffer. The film stars Tom Hulce as Mozart, Elizabeth Berridge as Constanze and F. Murray Abraham as Salieri.

Although some original documentary material was used as a basis for the plot, most Mozart experts agree that the story told in both the stage and cinema versions of *Amadeus* has been exaggerated and changed for dramatic effect. It's still a cracking film that races along, but if you compare it to our story of Mozart's life in the earlier chapters of this book, you will notice some important differences.

Amadeus is full of Mozart's hits including:
Gran partita, adagio
Piano Concerto No. 20, 2nd movement
Requiem
Symphony No. 25, 1st movement
Symphony No. 29, 1st movement

The following is a selection of other popular movies featuring the music of Mozart:

Ace Ventura, Pet Detective: Eine kleine Nachtmusik,
    2nd and 3rd movements

American Gigolo: Clarinet Concerto, 2nd movement

A Beautiful Mind: Piano Sonata No. 11

The Big Lebowski: Requiem

Educating Rita: Piano Concerto No. 21

Elvira Madigan: Piano Concerto No. 21, 2nd
    movement

Eye For An Eye: Clarinet Concerto, 2nd movement

Fame: Eine kleine Nachtmusik, 1st movement; *Piano*
    Sonata No. 11, 2nd movement

The French Lieutenant's Woman: Piano Sonata
    No. 15, 2nd movement

G.I. Jane: Adagio and Fugue, K456; *Eine kleine*
    Nachtmusik, 1st movement

Green Card: Clarinet Concerto, 2nd movement; *Flute*
    Concerto No. 1; Flute and Harp Concerto

JFK: Horn Concerto No. 2, 2nd movement

The Last Action Hero: Overture to *The Marriage of*
    Figaro

The Living Daylights: Symphony No. 40,
    1st movement

Lorenzo's Oil: Ave verum corpus

Me, Myself, I: Violin Concerto No. 5

My Left Foot: "Un' aura amorosa" from *Così fan tutte*

Nikita: Eine kleine Nachtmusik, 1st movement

Out Of Africa: Clarinet Concerto, 2nd movement

Philadelphia: "Agnus Dei" and "Dona nobis pacem"
    from *Coronation Mass;* "Laudate Dominum"

Primal Fear: "*Lacrymosa*" from *Requiem*

Runaway Bride: Overture to *The Marriage of Figaro*

Shakespeare's Romeo + Juliet: Symphony No. 25,
   1st movement

The Shawshank Redemption: "*Duettino sull*'" aria
   from *The Marriage of Figaro*

Star Trek: Insurrection: String Quartet No. 17,
   "*The Hunt*", 1st movement

Sunday, Bloody Sunday: "*Soave sia il vento*" from
   Così fan tutte

*There's Something About Mary: Eine kleine
   Nachtmusik*

Trading Places: Overture to *The Marriage of Figaro*

The Truman Show: Horn Concerto No. 1, 1st
   movement; *Piano Sonata No. 11,* 3rd movement

Who's That Girl?: Eine kleine Nachtmusik

The Whole Nine Yards: Eine kleine Nachtmusik

10

What the Others Said About Mozart

By and large, composers tend to be a rather fickle bunch and never miss the opportunity to stab one another in the back. However, many of the greatest composers through classical music history have been completely united in their praise for Mozart's music.

He is the greatest composer known to me either in person or by name.

JOSEPH HAYDN

Beethoven is the greatest composer – but Mozart is the only one.

GIOACCHINO ROSSINI

What gives Johann Sebastian Bach and Mozart a place apart is that these two great expressive composers never sacrificed form to expression. As high as their expression may soar, their musical form remains supreme and all-sufficient.

CAMILLE SAINT-SAËNS

Music must be set free from any sort of scientific approach; its aim must simply be to give pleasure. Within these limits it is possible to achieve great beauty. Extreme complication is the antithesis of art. Beauty must be something that can be felt, the pleasure it gives must be immediate; it must impose itself on us, or insinuate its way into us, without our having to make the least effort to reach out towards it. Look at Leonardo, look at Mozart. There were two great artists!

CLAUDE DEBUSSY

O Mozart, immortal Mozart, what countless images of a brighter and better world thou hast stamped upon our souls!

FRANZ SCHUBERT

*What Mozart composed up to his thirty-
sixth year, the best copyist of today could
not write down in the same amount of
time.*

Franz Strauss

---

*I like to play Bach, because it is
interesting to play a good fugue; but I do
not regard him, in common with many
others, as a great genius. Handel is only
fourth-rate, he is not even interesting.
I sympathize with Gluck in spite of his
poor creative gift. I also like some things
of Haydn. These four great masters have
been surpassed by Mozart. They are
rays which are extinguished by Mozart's
sun.*

Peter Ilyich Tchaikovsky

---

*Where the latter [Beethoven] is obscure
and seems to lack unity, the cause is not
the supposed rather wild originality for
which he is esteemed; it is that he turns
his back on eternal principles. Mozart
never does this. Each voice in Mozart has
its own line which, while according
perfectly with the other voices, forms its
own melody which follows in the most
perfect manner.*

Frédéric Chopin

Play Mozart in memory of me.

FRÉDÉRIC CHOPIN (HIS LAST WORDS)

Mozart!

GUSTAV MAHLER (HIS LAST WORD)

Where to Find Out More

There are a plethora of different books that have been written about Mozart's life and music. This *Friendly Guide* is by no means intended to be the definitive work on the subject, but we hope that it is has provided you with a good grounding in all things Mozartian. If we have whetted your appetite and you want to find out more about the man, as well as his music, here are a few pointers.

If you are looking for as near as possible a contemporaneous account of his life then, the first major biography of Mozart was written back in 1798 by Franz Xaver Niemetschek. It was based on

original documents provided for him by Mozart's wife, Constanze. The first biography in English came almost half a century later from Edward Holmes, in 1845.

For our money, the very best Mozart books have been written or edited by the great Mozart scholar, H.C. Robbins Landon. We would heartily recommend *The Mozart Compendium: A Guide to Mozart's Life and Music* published by Thames & Hudson in 1990. His other excellent books about Mozart include: *1791: Mozart's Last Year* (1988), *Mozart and Vienna* (1990), *Mozart: The Golden Years* (1991) and *The Mozart Essays* (1995).

If you would like to learn more about the subject of classical music in general, then *The DK Eyewitness Companion to Classical Music*, edited by John Burrows, is an excellent place to start. For a walk on the quirkier side of the subject, our own book *Classic Ephemera*, published by Boosey & Hawkes, is packed full of entertaining facts and stats from the world of classical music.

"The Mozart Effect" is a growing school of scientific thought that suggests that Mozart's music can improve intelligence. It follows on from an experiment on students at the University of California, the details of which were published in 1993.

The researchers found that listening to ten minutes of Mozart's piano music significantly improved performance in intelligence tests taken immediately afterwards. Scientists played the students a recording of Mozart's *Sonata for Two Pianos in D major*. Their results were significantly better than the same students achieved after a period of silence or after listening to a voice on a tape telling them to imagine themselves relaxing.

One of the scientists who has undertaken much of the research on the subject, Gordon L. Shaw, develops the ideas behind the Mozart Effect in his book *Keeping Mozart in Mind*, published by Elsevier Academic Press. This is definitely better suited to the more scientifically minded reader, but for the generalist, there is no better place to look than the logically titled *The Mozart Effect* by Don Campbell, published by Hodder & Stoughton.

For up-to-the-minute news on the latest recordings of Mozart's music, check out the magazines *Classic FM* and *Gramophone*, both of which are published monthly and carry extensive reviews of new CD releases. For concert information, check out www.classicfm.com.

The "Mostly Mozart" concert series, which originated in New York, takes place at the Barbican concert hall in London every summer. This festival combines Mozart's music with that of his

contemporaries, all performed by world-class soloists and orchestras.

If you are planning to travel to Salzburg, then make sure you pack a copy of the *Salzburg Insight Compact Guide* and the *Salzburg Insight Flexi Map* in your rucksack (both are published by Insight Compact Guides). For more details of Austria in general, we recommend *The Rough Guide to Austria*, edited by Jonathan Bousfield and Rob Humphreys, and *Essential Austria*, by Des Harrison (part of the AA Essential Series).

Mozart Mood Chart

Seriously raise your blood pressure

Seriously lower your blood pressure

A Musical Joke (fourth mvt)

Eine kleine Nachtmusik (first mvt)

Horn Concerto No. 2 (third mvt)

Flute and Harp Concerto (first mvt)

Der Hölle Rache kocht in meinem Herzen
(one of the Queen of the Night's arias in The Magic Flute)

Haffner Serenade (first mvt)

The Champagne Aria
(Don Giovanni)

Symphony No.40 (first mvt)

Overture to Così fan tutte

Overture to The Marriage of Figaro

Voi che sapete
(from The Marriage of Figaro)

Der Vogelfänger bin ich, ja
(the Birdcatcher aria from The Magic Flute)

Dove sono
(from The Marriage of Figaro)

Jupiter Symphony (fourth mvt)

Exsultate Jubilate

Non più andrai
(from the Marriage of Figaro)

Overture to Don Giovanni

Là ci darem la mano
(from Don Giovanni)

Laudate Dominum
(from the Solemn Vespers)

Ave Verum

Rondo alla Turca
(from Piano Sonata)

Symphony No.29
(first mvt)

Horn Concerto No.4 (third mvt)

Porgi Amor
(sung by The Countess in the Marriage of Figaro)

Eine kleine Nachtmusik
(second mvt)

Piano Concerto No.21 (second mvt)

Symphony No.40 (fourth mvt)

Clarinet Concerto (first mvt)

Soave sia il vento
(from Così fan tutte)

Clarinet Concerto
(second mvt)

Clarinet Quintet (second mvt)

Index

Allegri, Gregorio 67
Amsterdam 5, 43
Antwerp 4, 5, 43
Arco, Count Karl Joseph Felix 19, 89–90
Auernhammer, Josepha 96
Augsburg 8, 24, 35, 79, 87

Bach, C.P.E. 41
Bach, J.C. 19, 41
Bach, J.S. 19, 41, 113
Baden 120–122
Barisani, Sigmund 101, 108
Beethoven, Ludwig van 12, 19, 82, 108, 169
Berlin 13, 112, 114
Bohemia 5, 53
Bologna 6, 68
Bondini, Pasquale 108
Brussels 4, 5, 36, 43

Calais 4, 43
Canterbury 4, 42

Charlotte, Queen 41, 42, 46
Clementi, Muzio 10, 93
Colloredo, Prince Archbishop 10, 16, 19–20, 28, 72–78 *passim*, 83–88 *passim*, 92
Conti, Prince Louis Joseph de 44

Da Ponte, Lorenzo 17, 104, 108, 113, 169
Dijon 5, 45
Dover 4, 42
Dresden 13, 112

Eyck, Count Maximilian Emanuel Franz von 37

Firmian, Count Carl Joseph 65
Florence 6, 65, 66
Frankfurt 4, 14, 36, 116

Galitzin, Prince Dmitry Michailovich 20, 55, 56
George III, King 4, 39

Gluck, Christoph Willibald von 58, 65, 82
Gemmingen, Otto von 102

Haffner, Marie Elisabeth 78
Haffner, Siegmund 78, 95
Hagenauer, Johann Lorenz, 20, 52, 60
Hague, The 4, 43
Handel, Georg Frideric 39, 115
Haydn, Joseph 10, 17, 102–107 *passim*; Haydn, Michael 176
Hofmann, Leopold 119
Hoffmeister, Franz 105
Hulce, Tom 15, 178

Innsbruck 5, 61

Joseph I, Emperor 54
Joseph II, Emperor 14, 103, 106, 113–114

Koblenz 36–37
Künigl, Count 61

Lausanne 5
Leipzig 13, 112–113
Leopold II, Emperor 14, 66, 115
Leutgeb, Joseph 18, 52
Lichnowsky, Prince Karl 112
Lille 4, 43
Linz 99
London 4, 19, 38, 40, 41, 42
Lotter, Johann 24
Louis XV, King 4, 37, 54
Lugiati, Pietro 63
Luis I, King 54
Lyon 5

Mainz 14
Mannheim 8, 80–83, 116
Marie Antoinette 32, 49
Maximillian Joseph III, Elector 32
Mesmer, Dr Franz 58, 74
Metastasio, Pietro 72
Milan 6, 64, 68–70
Mozart, Anna Maria (daughter) 113
Mozart, Carl Thomas 101, 107, 116, 120

Mozart, Constanze (nee Weber) 10–17 *passim*, 92, 108–109, 175, 178, 186; marriage and children 94–99, 101, 107–116 *passim*, 120–122, 126–127, 131–133
Mozart, Franz Xaver Wolfgang 120
Mozart, Johann Thomas Leopold 107
Mozart, Leopold 12, 16, 20, 78–81, 83, 87, 92–95, 99, 102–103, 109; family background 23–30 *passim*; Wolfgang's career 34–47 *passim*, 50–61 *passim*, 63, 65, 68, 71–72, 76, 97, 105–108
Mozart, Maria Anna (mother) 17, 23, 25–26, 82–83
Mozart, Maria Anna Thekla (Bäsle) 79–80
Mozart, Nannerl (Maria Anna, sister) 4, 16, 25–29 *passim*, 53, 61, 76, 87, 100, 106–108; performing with Mozart 35–36, 42–49 *passim*, 54, 56
Mozart, Raimund Leopold 98–99, 101
Mozart, Theresia 110–111
Munich 4–9 *passim*, 14, 32–35 *passim*, 45, 76, 79, 83, 86–87, 116

Naples 6, 67

Olomouc 53

Paisiello, Giovanni 101
Petran, Franz 103
Paradies, Maria Theresia von 59
Paris 4–5, 8, 36–37, 44–45, 81–83
Piccinni, Niccolò 82
Potsdam 13, 112
Prague 12–13, 108, 111, 127–129, 145
Pressburg 33
Puchberg, Michael 18, 110–119 *passim*

Rauzzini, Venanzio 6, 20, 73, 174
Rome 6, 66

Salieri, Antonio 18, 124–125, 128–131 *passim*, 178

Salzburg 3, 5–9, 12, 23–28 *passim*, 30, 33–35, 43–46 *passim*, 51–52, 57, 60, 63, 70–78 *passim*, 80–88 *passim*, 97, 99, 102, 104, 127, 167

Sammartini, Giovanni Battista 64, 66

Schikaneder, Emanuel 129, 130

Shaffer, Peter 62, 178

Schrattenbach, Prince Archbishop 20, 28, 52–53, 60–62, 71, 84

Spitzeder, Franz Anton 20, 52

Stadler, Anton 13, 19, 164, 170

Stoll, Anton 120, 122

Strasbourg 8

Süssmayr, Franz Xaver 21, 127

Swieten, Baron von 115

Telemann, Georg Phillipp 26

Utrecht 5, 43

Verona 5–6, 61, 63–64, 70

Vienna 5–6, 11–12, 14, 20, 32–35 *passim*, 53–59, 88, 91–99 *passim*, 101–113 *passim*, 118–119, 122–123, 129, 131, 136, 150, 157

Venice 6, 70

Wagenseil, Georg Christoph 3, 29, 39

Walsegg–Stuppach, Count Franz von 124–125, 164

Weber, Aloysia 8, 10, 80–83 *passim*, 92

Weber Fridolin 80, 92

Weiser, Anton 21, 52

Williamson, Thomas 38

Winter, Sebastian 35

Zurich 5

About the Authors

Darren Henley is the Station Manager of Classic FM. His radio programmes have been honoured by the Sony Radio Academy Awards, the British Radio Awards, the New York International Radio Festival and the United Nations. He writes regularly for *Classic FM* magazine. Previously a journalist for Invicta Radio in Kent and for ITN, he is the co-author of autobiographies of Aled Jones and the band G4, both published by Virgin Books. He has written three Naxos audiobooks for children, one of which, *The Story of Classical Music*, was nominated for a Grammy Award, named as best original work by the American Audiobook Publishers Association and won the *Radio Times* Readers' Choice Award at the British Spoken Word Awards in 2005.

Tim Lihoreau is the Creative Director of Classic FM. He studied music at the University of Leeds and worked as a professional pianist before joining Jazz FM, from where he moved to Classic FM. He has been responsible for writing and producing many of the station's most acclaimed programmes, which have been honoured by the Sony Radio Academy Awards, the NTL Commercial Radio Awards and the New York International Radio Festival. His column "Modern Phobias" has appeared regularly in the *Daily Telegraph* and his books include *Stephen Fry's Incomplete and Utter History of Classical Music*, published by Macmillan.

The Classic FM Friendly Guide to Mozart is the fifth book about classical music that Darren Henley and Tim Lihoreau have written together.